Luke IN THE Land

Lifeway Press®
Brentwood, Tennessee

ISBN: 978-1-0877-8894-4
Item: 005843027
Dewey decimal classification: 225.9
Subject heading: BIBLE. N.T. LUKE \ BIBLE--GEOGRAPHY \ BIBLE--HISTORY OF BIBLICAL EVENTS

To order additional copies of this resource, write Lifeway Resources Customer Service; 200 Powell Place, Suite 100; Brentwood, TN 37027-7707; Fax order to 615.251.5933; call toll-free 800.458.2772; email orderentry@lifeway.com; or order online at lifeway.com.

Printed in the United States of America.

Lifeway Women Bible Studies
Lifeway Resources
200 Powell Place, Suite 100
Brentwood, TN 37027-7707

EDITORIAL TEAM, LIFEWAY WOMEN BIBLE STUDIES

Becky Loyd
Director, Lifeway Women

Tina Boesch
Manager

Chelsea Waack
Production Leader

Elizabeth Hyndman
Content Editor

Sarah Kilgore
Production Editor

Lauren Ervin
Graphic Designer

Table of Contents

About the Author

KRISTI MCLELLAND is a speaker, teacher, and college professor. Since completing her Master of Arts in Christian Education at Dallas Theological Seminary, she has dedicated her life to discipleship, to teaching people how to study the Bible for themselves, and to writing about how God is better than we ever knew by explaining the Bible through a Middle Eastern lens. She has written two other Bible studies: *Jesus and Women* focuses on Jesus's earthly ministry and His interactions with first-century women, while *The Gospel on the Ground* follows the early church through the book of Acts. Her great desire for people to truly experience the love of God birthed a ministry in which she leads biblical study trips to Israel, Turkey, Greece, and Italy.

For more information about Kristi and what she's up to, visit: newlensbiblicalstudies.com.

From the Author

On October 7, 2023, I was sitting in a restaurant in the Newark airport, enjoying a cheese plate and waiting for my flight to Tel Aviv, Israel. I anticipated joining up with over three hundred people for our biblical study trip together with Lifeway. As I waited, my phone lit up, notifying me that my flight to Tel Aviv had been canceled due to "unrest in the region." My heart seized. I knew something had gone terribly wrong. I will never forget that helpless, heartbroken, and gutted feeling as I sat in the airport—now waiting for my flight to take me back to Tennessee.

News outlets have reported that October 7, 2023 was the bloodiest day for Jewish people since the Holocaust. It has been referred to as "Israel's 9/11." In the days following October 7, I felt such deep grief and lament, shock and disbelief—a profound sadness I could feel in my very bones.

I started thinking about the fact that one month earlier, in September of 2023, I was IN Israel with the Lifeway video team as we filmed all of the teachings you will experience in this 7-session series. That filming project was a stretch for me in so many ways. It was a hard *yes* to give because my heart is to take people to Israel.

But the Lord has been impressing upon my heart over the last few years (since COVID-19) that I need to bring Israel here more and more. This has been a hard thing for me to submit to as I love being in Israel more than anything else.

I submitted to the adventure of writing *Luke in the Land*, and I reluctantly submitted to filming the teachings in Israel. But the true surrender to it has come since October 7. With COVID and now the events of October 7 and following, I'm surrendered to this adventure of trying my best to bring Israel here more and more. My heart feels both agreement and yielding to be more open to these things.

Tragedy sometimes works in strange ways as it changes us, diverts us, and often moves us into new creative and innovative adventures. Pain in the hands of God will be turned into beautiful things if we will let it. I had some surprising and absolutely beautiful moments while we were filming these teachings in Israel.

We started with a sunrise filming on the Arbel Cliffs, overlooking the Sea of Galilee. While I was filming on the Mount of Olives at sunset, a guy kept yelling "Shakira!" at me. I visited the ancient Emmaus Road for the very first time and walked on it as we filmed. It's a portion of that ancient road that Jesus walked with two disappointed disciples after His resurrection (Luke 24). I have sat in many places where Jesus would've sat, but walking a road that resurrected Jesus walked just about did me in.

I could go on and on, but delight and joy and wonder found me during this filming project. I would not have experienced these things without first giving a submitted *yes* to it.

Sitting here writing this, I can actually say that this *Luke in the Land* study is given with my fully submitted and surrendered heart to you and yours. I hope you love getting to know Jesus better not only in His first-century Jewish world, but in the land of Israel where He lived, ministered, died, resurrected, and ascended.

Kristi McLelland

How to Use This Study

In our time together, we are going to glimpse some snapshots of the story of Jesus in the land where He walked. We are going to study God's Word in a way that might seem a bit different from what you've experienced in the past. The Gospel of Luke is written in a way similar to how you might scrapbook or pick out photos for an album—one snapshot at a time. We'll be looking at four snapshots in the life of Jesus each session.

LEADING A GROUP?

A free leader guide PDF is available for download at lifeway.com/lukeintheland. The leader guide offers several tips and helps, along with discussion guides for each week.

Scan me

Resources are available to help you promote the study in your church or neighborhood, including: invitation card, promotional poster, bulletin insert, and PowerPoint® template. You'll find these and more at lifeway.com/lukeintheland.

▶ WHAT'S INSIDE

The **SNAPSHOT** sections are for your personal study time. Instead of labeling them by days of study, we've labeled them as snapshots, taking from the structure of the Gospel of Luke itself. Feel free to complete each between our weekly group times as you see fit throughout the week.

The **WATCH AND DISCUSS** times are meant to be completed with your small group. In the Middle Eastern way, the original context of the Gospel of Luke, learning is very communal. Here's what I mean: in a Middle Eastern context, it would be common to see rabbis teaching students as they walked down the road. This teaching tradition places significant value on students discussing an issue with one another.

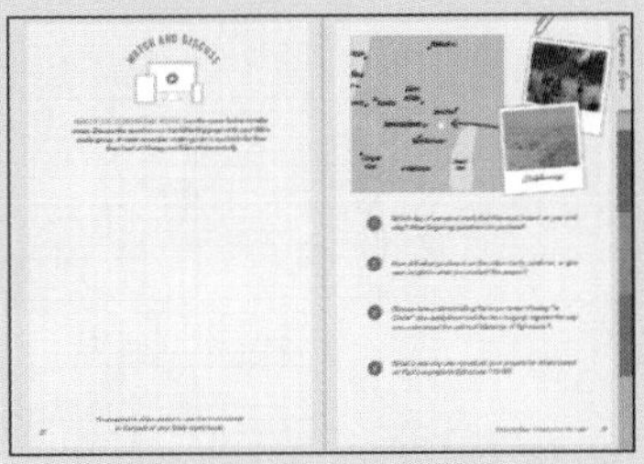

You'll notice group discussion guides crafted especially for you to use as you yeshiva, or discuss biblical text together, after you've studied them throughout the week. You'll also find a place for you to take notes as you watch the week's teaching video.

VIDEO ACCESS: You'll find detailed information for how to access the video teaching sessions that accompany this study on the card inserted in the back of your Bible study book.

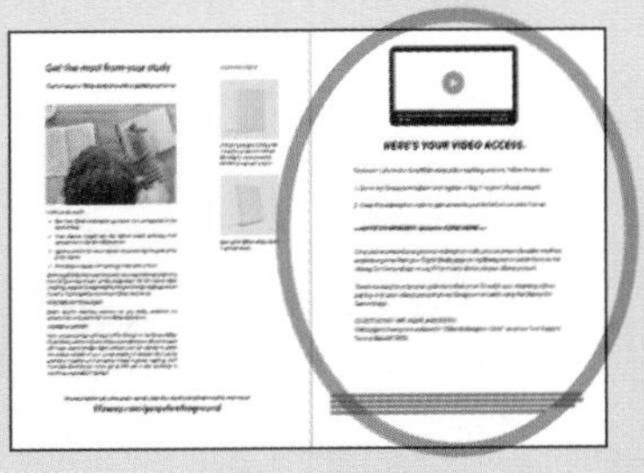

LOOKING FOR MORE? Watch the optional bonus video from Kristi, "The Making of Luke in the Land," available on the Lifeway On Demand app or lifeway.com/lukeintheland. In the video, Kristi shares a bit more of her heart behind the study and how God used the teaching in Israel in her own life.

Session One

Introduction to LUKE

ANSWER THE FOLLOWING QUESTIONS:

Before you start this study, I've provided some prompts for reflection and discussion to help ready you for our journey together over the next several weeks.

1. I'm here because my heart needs . . .

2. Where would you want to visit in Israel? Why?

3. With whom in Luke's Gospel would you want to have coffee? What would you want to discuss?

4. If you could go back in a time machine and witness any story or event that takes place in the Gospels, which one would it be? Why?

SNAPSHOT 1

Introduction to Luke

Jerome (AD 347–420), an early church father from Croatia, moved to Bethlehem and gave almost forty decades of his life to translating the biblical texts from the original languages of Hebrew and Greek into Latin. He contributed to a translation called the Latin Vulgate, which the church used for about a thousand years as a primary translation of the Bible.[1] St. Jerome is commonly believed to have said that there is a "fifth Gospel."

> Five Gospels record the life of Jesus. Four you will find in books and the one you will find in the land they call Holy. Read the fifth Gospel and the world of the four will open to you.
>
> **COMMONLY ATTRIBUTED TO ST. JEROME**

In other words, the land of Israel is the "fifth Gospel" accompanying the four we read. The land is the "Gospel" we walk. We take in the biblical four by reading, but we experience the "fifth" with our five senses.

READ LUKE 1:1-4. **What wording does Luke use to describe the life of Jesus in verse 1?**

In verse 4, why does he say he is writing the Gospel account?

As the author of the third Gospel, Luke had lived and walked the "fifth Gospel." He interviewed eyewitnesses to the life, ministry, death, and resurrection of Jesus and sat down to write his Gospel—the Gospel of Luke from these accounts. Luke's Gospel reminds me of a photo album full of snapshots.

We don't take and collect photos of every single moment of our lives (such as shopping on aisle three at Target®, taking out the trash, picking up kids from school, sitting in a doctor's office, packing for a trip, etc.). But we do take photos to remember significant moments—important moments lived with the people we lived them alongside (school, holidays, babies, birthday parties, graduations, weddings, vacations, beautiful sunsets that made us cry, etc.)

I could get a really good sense of who you are, whom you love, what you care about, and the world that has shaped you and your worldview simply by looking at your photo albums and your snapshots—the snapshots you chose to keep along the way.

What are some of your favorite snapshots or stories in your own life?

Who's in your photo albums?

What places are in your photo albums?

Similar to our photo albums, in the Gospel of Luke every single moment is not recorded. Every single story is not told. Every miracle, or teaching, or city visited by Jesus is not recorded. Rather, Luke told the stories he learned and heard from others. He provides gospel-gorgeous snapshots of the gospel story. The full testimony of Jesus could never be fully captured in human words in any one Gospel account. The very last verse of the very last Gospel, John's Gospel, ends with this truth.

> Jesus did many other things as well.
> If every one of them were written down,
> I suppose that even the whole world would
> not have room for the books that would be written.
> **JOHN 21:25**

Have you ever thought of the Bible and the Gospels in this way? What are some of your favorite "snapshots" from Scripture? From Jesus's life?

Prompted by the Holy Spirit, Luke recorded the exact stories the living God wanted us to have. This makes me want to EAT my Bible and carry it around inside me. I want to see the snapshots He wants me to have, to hold, to carry within me as I live, move, and have my being in this life.

We are a people who are meant to experience Jesus. The four written Gospels and the "fifth Gospel" of the land of Israel invite us to experience Jesus and to understand Him in His first-century world—His life, ministry, crucifixion, and resurrection—so that we might follow Him, being like Him in our own world.

LUKE: BACKGROUND & STORY-TELLING

Luke's Gospel is the third of four Gospels located in the canon of the New Testament. However, originally it was seen as part one of a two-volume work that included the book of Acts.[2] We can easily forget this point because the placement of John's Gospel as the fourth separates Luke's Gospel account from his further writings that follow in Acts. The earliest readers of the text would have read Luke and Acts as one continuous story. What began in Luke would see fulfillment throughout Acts and on and on until this very moment you and I find ourselves in. We too are part of this story.

The original work, known as Luke-Acts, makes up approximately one-fourth of the entire New Testament![3] We don't often think of Luke as one of the most prolific contributors to the New Testament writings, but with 24 chapters in Luke and 28 chapters in Acts, his literary contribution is a substantial gift to us who feast on the life, ministry, stories, and kingdom work of Jesus and His earliest disciples.

The Gospels and Acts are first-century teaching documents, rather than personal correspondence like much of the rest of the New Testament. As such, these texts do not provide Luke's name as the author. However, reliable early Christian sources, such as the M. Canon (AD 170) and writings from Iranaeus (AD 180), confirm Luke as the writer of Luke-Acts.[4]

What do you know about Luke, the person?

READ COLOSSIANS 4:14; 2 TIMOTHY 4:9-11; AND PHILEMON 23-24. **What do you learn about Luke?**

Luke was most likely a Gentile physician, well-versed in Greek culture and language, a follower of Jesus, and a companion of Paul on some of his missionary journeys and adventures. Paul refers to him as "dear friend Luke, the doctor" (Col. 4:14) and as a "fellow worker" (Philem. 24).

While Luke is not specifically mentioned as the author of Luke-Acts, one unique feature of Luke's Gospel is that it is the only one that names its recipient—"most excellent Theophilus," and "Theophilus" (Luke 1:3; Acts 1:1). Theophilus means "beloved by God." The phrase "most excellent" indicates that he was most likely a person of high social rank and financial status. We see this term used of other upper echelon people in the book of Acts (23:26; 24:3; 26:25). Theophilus was most likely the literary patron who financially provided for the copying of these Luke-Acts scrolls for himself and others.[5]

LUKE 1:1-4	Josephus's similar introduction in *Against Apion*
"Many have undertaken to draw up an account of the things that have been fulfilled among us, just as they were handed down to us by those who from the first were eyewitnesses and servants of the word. With this in mind, since I myself have carefully investigated everything from the beginning, I too decided to write an orderly account for you, most excellent Theophilus, so that you may know the certainty of the things you have been taught."	"In the former book, most excellent Epaphroditus, I have demonstrated our antiquity, and confirmed the truth of what I have said, from the writings of the Phoenicians, and Chaldeans, and Egyptians. I have, moreover, produced many of the Grecian writers as witnesses thereto."[6]

We often do not think of Luke as the one who wrote one-fourth of the New Testament, and we certainly don't think of Theophilus as being the financier of one-fourth of the New Testament! The partnership between these two men giving what they had to further the story of the gospel being written and shared moves me deeply. Luke was educated and fluent in the Greek language, while Theophilus was a Jesus-follower with bank! One gave his reed pen or metal stylus to write it. One gave his money to pay for it.

And here we are, two thousand years later, *still* reading the gospel-gorgeous story of Jesus and His followers that those two wrote and financed. This reminds me of a simple principle I try to live by as a follower of Jesus:

GIVE WHAT YOU GOT!

When have you seen fellow believers "giving what they got" to further the message of Jesus?

How might you be called to "give what you got" (use your talents and treasures) to share the story of Jesus with others?

It is beautiful to imagine Luke, some two thousand years ago, writing the third Gospel as he walked the "fifth Gospel," interviewing eyewitnesses to the life and ministry of Jesus and the early church and scribing these stories as the Holy Spirit led him (Luke 1:1-4). In Acts 27:1 and Acts 28:1, Luke used the word *we*, indicating that he was with Paul in Jerusalem and Caesarea during that two-and-a-half-year time frame. This would have most likely been the time Luke interviewed his eyewitnesses and wrote his Gospel account, even as he was walking, embodying, seeing, and experiencing the land of Israel for himself.[7]

✱ Jerusalem as it appears today

SNAPSHOT 2

Historical Context

> In the time of Herod the king of Judea . . .
> **LUKE 1:5a**

> In those days Caesar Augustus . . .
> **LUKE 2:1a**

Have you ever thought about the timing of Jesus's birth into the world? Every Christmas season we celebrate His birth, the beautiful story told in Matthew 1–2 and Luke 2—when the living God took on flesh and broke into human history, changing it forever. What was the world Jesus was born into like, and what can we learn about Him from both the timing and the context of His incarnational arrival?

CONTEXT

The Bible tells an ongoing story about the people of Israel and the people groups and nations they interacted with. The Israelites were often subjected to foreign rule and oppression—empires that came and went, taking everything they could along the way. The list goes something like this: Egypt (Ex.), Assyria (2 Kings 17), Babylon (Dan.), Persia (Esth., Neh.), Greece (Intertestamental Period), and Rome (New Testament).

Within these difficult stories of harsh domination by cruel pharaohs, kings, and caesars, there are stories of light in the darkness, hope in the midst of despair, and of salvation and deliverance. These biblical stories teach us to look for light in our own darkness, to reach for hope in our own despair, and to courageously cry out for salvation and deliverance in our own lives.

The overarching narrative of the Bible is localized among those who are on the bottom of society's hierarchies and structures. Jesus, the King of kings, came all the way to the lowest circle of humanity, found the lost, the sick, and the marginalized, and prioritized them.

LOOK UP LUKE 4:18-21 AND LUKE 19:10. **What does this tell you about Jesus's mission on earth?**

No "king" had ever done this in human history.

Between the Old Testament and New Testament, there was a time period called the Intertestamental Period. It covered approximately four hundred years between Malachi, the last book of the Old Testament, and Matthew, the first book of the New Testament. Significant changes impacted the whole world during this time. Those changes came when the Greeks, through Alexander the Great, emerged as the ruling superpower in the earth. *Koine* or "common" Greek became the *lingua franca,* and Greek culture (Hellenism) was systematically spread through the kingdoms conquered by the Greeks. Alexander wanted the whole world to be Greek, and he was well on his way to achieving his goals when he died in his early thirties.[8]

* The Alexander Mosaic is a Roman floor mosaic originally from the House of the Faun in Pompeii.

As we move closer to the world at the time of Jesus's birth, we come to a very important date during the Intertestamental Period, one that set the stage for the context of the Gospels in the New Testament. In 63 BC a Roman general named Pompey conquered Judea and Jerusalem, like others who had come before him. He laid siege to Jerusalem and eventually broke into the city. Twelve thousand Jewish people died in Jerusalem that day.

* Tetradrachm of Alexander the Great

But Pompey took it one step further. Ancient Jewish historian Josephus reported that Pompey entered the temple, even entered as far as the Holy of Holies—something the high priest of Israel did only once a year on the Day of Atonement.[9]

Pompey looked around but did not touch the temple furnishings or treasures. His disregard for temple order and sacredness was the ultimate sacrilege for the Jewish people. His actions served as a sign of what life under Roman rule would look like for years to come, as the Roman Empire exerted its dominance from 63 BC, through the New Testament era, and beyond. The Jewish people likely recognized Rome as the new enemy.

READ ABOUT THE DAY OF ATONEMENT IN LEVITICUS 16:2-4. **How does this passage inform on the inappropriateness of Pompey's actions?**

✱ Caesar Augustus

TIMING

Julius Caesar, another formidable Roman general and statesman, defeated Pompey in 48 BC, and declared himself as the dictator of Rome for life.[10] Before he was famously assassinated in 44 BC, he was deified as a god. Later, as Rome transitioned from a republic to an empire in 27 BC, Caesar's adopted son, Gaius Octavian, secured sole rulership as the first true emperor, or Caesar, of the Roman Empire. The Senate conferred the name "Augustus" or "revered one" on him and he was known as Caesar Augustus.[11]

Believed to have divine origins, Augustus was identified by the Latin phrase *divi filius*, or "son of god."[12] It was this Caesar who was enthroned in imperial Rome when Jesus, the true Son of God, was birthed in lowly Bethlehem. These names and events start to bring the timing of Jesus's earthly arrival into focus. When man became a god, God became a man.

Caesar Augustus ruthlessly squashed civil wars within the empire and inaugurated the *Pax Romana*—"Roman peace." This "peace" lasted for approximately two hundred years and permeated the environment into which Jesus was born. Unlike the peace associated with Hebrew *shalom*—lovely, calm, and universally beneficial peace—this Roman peace held more oppressive connotations. This was a "peace" maintained at all costs by the heavy hand of Rome. It benefited those on top and in power at the expense of those below and on the margins of society.[13]

✱ Aerial view of Caesarea with its ruins and antiquities. In the middle is the hippodrome where horse chariot races took place.

While Caesar Augustus ruled the Roman Empire and the world, Herod the Great was installed as a local king in Judea—the king of the Jews. As a personal friend of the famed couple Mark Antony and Cleopatra VII of Egypt, Herod governed at the time of Jesus's birth. However, he served as more of a puppet king, installed by the Romans to keep the peace in the seemingly insignificant Judean outpost.[14]

Herod was a paranoid, murderous ruler. He built magnificent structures, and even cities like Caesarea Maritima, to appease the Romans above him while he was mistrusted and even hated by his Jewish subjects. Herod had no fewer than three of his own sons killed, as well as his most beloved wife, Mariamne, a Hasmonean princess. Caesar Augustus was thought to have said of Herod that it was "safer to be Herod's pig (*hus*) than his son (*huios*)."[15] Knowing this, we are not surprised at the Massacre of the Innocents, an incident recorded in Matthew 2:16-18, when Herod ordered all boys aged two and under in the vicinity of Bethlehem to be murdered.

Whenever I think about the world Jesus was born into, I think about the familiar Christmas carol, "O Holy Night." The lyrics speak to the first Christmas as well as to ours, two thousand years later.

> Long lay the world
> in sin and error pining.
>
> Til he appeared
> and the soul felt its worth.[16]
>
> **O HOLY NIGHT**

✱ Caesarea as it appears today

SNAPSHOT 3

Good News for All People

The world was dark indeed during this time in human history. It is interesting to me that Luke uses the word and concept of a *soter*—"savior" throughout his Gospel.[17]

Look up the times Luke uses the word *savior* and take note of the context each time. Who is using the word? What were the circumstances?

Luke 1:47

Luke 2:11

While all the Gospels speak to Jesus as Savior, Matthew and Mark do not use the word *soter,* and John uses it only once. Luke is emphasizing this "Savior" coming into this world. His Gospel tells the story of the Son of God being born *while* the Roman "son of god," Augustus, was in power.

Jesus was born right under the nose of Herod the Great and within the Roman Empire of Caesar Augustus. A Judean king and a Caesar of empire ruled while the light of the world was coming into the world to be the Savior. Jesus would show that there is another way to order the world than the way of empire—the powerful lording over the powerless. Jesus would show the way of the kingdom of God right in the midst of empire. He would bring a gospel, good news for ALL people, not only for the few at the top.

The angels embodied this very reality when they served as divine heralds to Bethlehem shepherds. The good news was prioritized and given first to shepherds who were lowly and believed to be on the margins in their own culture. This "good news" was good news even for shepherds.

> But the angel said to them, "Do not be afraid. I bring you good news that will cause great joy for all the people. Today in the town of David a Savior has been born to you; he is the Messiah, the Lord."
> LUKE 2:10-11

READ LUKE 22:25-26. **Given the historical and cultural context you read in today's study, why was this statement especially radical? Would such a statement be radical in our current context? Why or why not?**

KINGDOM VERSUS EMPIRE

We know that Jesus's central teaching was the Sermon on the Mount, located in Matthew 5–7 and Luke 6:17-49. This is His longest recorded teaching in the Bible.

Throughout both the Sermon on the Mount and in His teaching and ministry as a Rabbi of Israel, He continually proclaimed one theme. What was that theme?

LOOK UP MATTHEW 4:17,23-25; LUKE 4:43; LUKE 10:1-9; ACTS 1:1-3. **What was Jesus proclaiming in all these verses?**

Jesus spoke over and over again about the kingdom of God. Dwight A. Pryor says it well:

> The importance of the Kingdom message for Jesus therefore can scarcely be overestimated. In his preaching, he proclaimed the Kingdom; in his teaching, he explained the Kingdom; in his parables, he illustrated the Kingdom; and in his healings and deliverances Jesus demonstrated the present, powerful and in-breaking Kingdom of Heaven.[18]

The *kingdom of God* or the *kingdom of heaven*—the two terms are interchangeable and mean the same thing. *Heaven* is something of an idiom for *God* to the Jewish people. Devout Jews do not speak the Divine Name of God that was spoken to Moses at the burning bush—*YHWH* (yud-heh-vav-heh in Hebrew). *HaShem* (The Name) is a common name used by devout Jews to say the name of the Lord. "Kingdom of heaven" is a way of saying "kingdom of God" without saying His Name.

In Hebrew, it is called the *malkhut shamayim*. Dr. Pryor explains that the phrase is a "verbal noun," meaning that it speaks of a present reality, not a future hope.[19]

What do you think the "kingdom of God" means?

Simply put, the *kingdom of God* is God's reign over the universe. He is sovereign and has dominion over everything in and under heaven. It's a term that's used in the Old Testament, but "arises more specifically from Jesus' proclamation of the inbreaking of God's rule."[20] And what is God's rule breaking in on? The empire.

Jesus's world in Luke, and our world today, was and is anchored in the way of the empire. We are striving orphans, starving and trying to acquire more and more and more. Jesus breaks in with a different way—the way of the kingdom.

How is our world today anchored in the way of the empire? Fill in the chart below with some examples of how the kingdom of God differs from the way of the empire. ***I've included one to get you started. As you continue your study of Luke, revisit this chart and add to it as a reminder of how Jesus brought in a radical new way.***

KINGDOM	EMPIRE
Striving	Sabbath/Rest

This concept of the inbreaking of God's rule was central to Jesus's teaching, so we'll keep encountering it as we walk through the land and through Luke's Gospel. We'll fill out this chart together as we go to learn more of what Jesus's heart and head and hands were working toward in His ministry on earth. You'll see how radical it was—and how radical it still is—to live the kingdom life in the world of the empire.

God's rule is breaking in. Let's go!

✱ Church of the Nativity, Bethlehem, Israel

SNAPSHOT 4

Advent

Advent is my absolute favorite time of year. It's the first season of the Christian calendar and covers the four Sundays preceding Christmas Day. Advent comes from the Latin word *adventus*, which means "arrival" or "coming."[21] It remembers and celebrates Jesus's first advent (birth), and it anticipates His second advent, the second coming of Christ.

As part of the New Testament church, we hold the privilege of all people in human history to live sandwiched between Jesus's two comings. We have the testimony of the four Gospels behind us as we look to the promised second coming in front of us. The Gospels of both Matthew and Luke include Advent—the birth story of Jesus and accounts of His earthly parents, Mary and Joseph.

Jesus's advent was different from the arrival of other kings throughout human history. Kings typically came and conquered. They entered cities with swords and armies. They brought imprisonment, subjugation, harsh taxation, and ruled with heavy hands and fists. They ruled from the top down, with power centralized at the top and everyone below used up for imperial expansion and progression.

Jesus's advent brought the beginning of a new way to order the world. His arrival ignited a gospel (good news) that would indeed be good news for ALL people. Jesus's advent ushered into the world the beginnings of a true peace, an ancient *shalom* that was prophesied by the prophet Isaiah.

READ ISAIAH 9:6-7. Which of these names and promises about Jesus do you think the people of the time were most excited about? What do you think they were looking for in the promised Messiah?

Which of the promises about the Messiah from Isaiah 9:6-7 brings you the most comfort?

This child was indeed born in Bethlehem in Judea, was raised in Nazareth, and lived as a grown man and rabbi of Israel in Capernaum, in the district of Galilee. But what did Jesus advent into the world to do? He answered this question in both word and deed throughout the four Gospels—with the Gospel of Luke being our focus in this biblical feast.

> For the Son of Man came to seek and save the lost.
> LUKE 19:10

Jesus came for lost humanity—to save us and bring us home. Have you ever been lost? The only thing worse than being lost is being lost and knowing that no one is coming for you.

Cell phones came out when I was a sophomore in college. My first "cell phone" was a bag phone that stayed in my car; I plugged it into the cigarette lighter and it was only used in the case of an emergency. It was the first time I ever felt I could reach out for help if I got lost on my way somewhere. Before the cell phone, if my car broke down and I was alone, I simply had to sit on the side of the road in rural Mississippi and hope for someone to drive by, stop, and help me. I can remember that gnawing feeling in my stomach of not knowing if anyone would come by to offer help.

Have you had a similar experience of being really lost? What did you feel when you realized you were lost?

As far back as Genesis 3, God has been about seeking and saving the lost.

READ GENESIS 3:8-10. Who asked the question in these verses?

Questions in the Bible are meaningful and often convey much more meaning than we interpret at first glance. They often answer things in a Near Eastern, Jewish way. Notice how many times Jesus answered a question with a question. In many gospel moments, His question *was* answering the question asked, and it ended the conversation (more on this later).

The first question the Lord ever asked in the Bible was in the garden of Eden after Adam and Eve ate the forbidden fruit. Cloaked in shame, they had hidden themselves among the trees when they heard the Lord walking through the garden in the cool of the day.

LOOK AT GENESIS 3:8-10 AGAIN. What was the first question God asked of man?

These three words in English are one word in Hebrew—*ayeka*.[22]

When you read this, how do you imagine hearing the tone in His voice? In your imagination, does he sound angry? Disappointed? Sad? Frantic?

Why do you imagine his voice and tone sounding that way?

I often imagine His voice sounding something like a mixture of sadness and hope all at once. Sad because they had broken *shalom*. Hopeful because He knew He could cover their shame (and He did, with animal skins). He was looking for them—not to kill them, but to save them. The Lord was looking to enter into their heartbreak so that He could begin the work of restoration.

The prophet Isaiah gave us this jewel about the living God's posture and movement toward us as lost humanity:

> Yet the LORD longs to be gracious to you;
> therefore he will rise up to show you compassion.
> **ISAIAH 30:18a**

What makes the living God rise up? What makes Him come close?

The word compassion is a fusion of two words—*com* (with) and *pathos* (pain). Compassion is not so much an emotion that we feel. Compassion is a location—we are compassionate when we locate ourselves with someone in his or her pain. The Lord looked for Adam and Eve in the garden to meet them in their pain. Most of all, I imagine *ayeka* with a tone of compassion.

Throughout the Gospel of Luke, we will see Jesus practicing compassion—locating Himself with people right in the middle of their pain. He sought out and found the lost and offered to bring them home. He does the same today. Jesus is not afraid of our sin or our pain; He meets us there and offers to bring us home.

Ayeka
"Where are you?"

We may feel lost from time to time, but we are never lost with no one coming for us. Rather, the living God still asks, *ayeka*, "Where are you?" We can afford to cry out, to wait on the Lord, to endure the present pain and trial. He is the one who advents, or comes, for us. Let us be found by Him anew today, right where we are.

What would it look like for you to invite God to locate Himself with you in your pain today?

Take a moment and praise God for His presence. Ask to feel His presence and compassion in your pain, or ask for His presence to be felt in the life of a loved one who is experiencing pain right now.

WATCH AND DISCUSS

WATCH THE SESSION ONE VIDEO. **Use the space below to take notes. Discuss the questions on the following page with your Bible study group. A more extensive leader guide is available for free download at lifeway.com/lukeintheland.**

To access the video sessions, use the instructions in the back of your Bible study book.

Wilderness

1. What are some of your favorite snapshots or stories in your own life? (Consider bringing in snapshots, or sharing photos from your phone with the group.)

2. When have you seen fellow believers "giving what they got" (using their talents and treasures) to share the story of Jesus with others?

3. What did you learn about the historical context into which Jesus was born? How does that speak to God's plan for His people?

4. Read Isaiah 9:6-7 as a group. Which of these names and promises about the Messiah brings you the most comfort right now? Why?

✱ Church of the Nativity,
Bethlehem, Israel

Session Two

INCARNATION

SNAPSHOT 1

A Portrait of Joseph

Of the four Gospels, Matthew and Luke give us the birth narratives of Jesus. Matthew gives the birth story through the eyes of Joseph. Luke gives the story through the eyes of Mary. Together, they tell a beautiful story of two people, Joseph and Mary, risking greatly as they answered the angelic invitations sent by God to be His vessels in bringing forth the long-awaited Messiah.

READ MATTHEW 1:18-25. **What do we know about Joseph from these verses?**

According to the Protoevangelium of James, a second-century extra canonical document, Joseph was an older widow with children when he was betrothed to Mary.[1] However, scholars debate the accuracy of this portrayal. The Mishnah, a sacred Jewish text, says that Jewish boys married around the age of eighteen.[2] Scripture itself does not tell us Joseph's age at his betrothal, and the Bible is silent regarding whether this is Joseph's first marriage. Whether Joseph was an older widower or a younger man at betrothal, his yes to God was risky.

What other risky *yeses* can you think of from the Bible?

Have you seen people in your life say yes to risky asks from God? Have you ever said a risky yes in obedience? Tell about one of those.

More about:

THE PROTO GOSPEL OF JAMES

The Proto Gospel of James (*Protoevangelium of James*) is an extracanonical second-century infancy gospel that tells the supposed miraculous story of Mary's unique birth to her mother Anna, the supposed birth of Jesus in a cave, Joseph as an older widow with children at the time of betrothal to Mary, and so on.4

✱ Sepphoris, with view of Nazareth in the distance

More about
MARRIAGE CONTRACTS

According to the *Ketubot* ("marriage documents") in the Mishnah, people did not choose one another to marry—the parents chose for them (arranged marriages).

The ***ketubah*** was a marriage contract submitted to the bride and her family by the groom. It outlined a widow-settlement to be paid to the women if the marriage dissolved either by divorce or death. If the bride's family agreed to the contract, the couple was officially betrothed.[7]

Betrothals generally lasted one year and ended with the bride being carried by litter or carriage to the groom's father's home while people celebrated, danced and played music in the streets. The bride most likely wore a "crown" of some type and was greeted by tambourines and drums by the groom and his father's family upon arrival. Then the groom's family hosted a wedding feast, which could last a week or so.

According to the Bible, Joseph was a carpenter (see Matt. 13:55). The Greek word used is *tekton*, which indicates he worked with stone and other building materials.[3] Based on his location, Joseph most likely walked the three to five miles from Nazareth to Sepphoris, a large Greco-Roman city, to be employed as a stonemason in building projects within that major city.

Jewish tradition identifies Joseph as a *tzaddik*, or as Matthew described him in Greek, *diakaios* (Matt. 1:19).[5] Both terms refer to a generous and righteous man. We see this clearly in his treatment of Mary when he found out that she was pregnant during their betrothal period. Betrothal was a legally binding marriage arrangement prior to the wedding, sexual consummation, and bride's return to the husband's family home with him. The betrothal contract was known as a *ketubah*, or a traditional Jewish marriage contract.[6]

Joseph lived in a world of economic injustice. He and his people lived under the heavy taxation policies of both Caesar Augustus and Herod the Great, the king of Judea. Joseph lived in a world where every denarii (one day's wage) counted. By bringing Mary before the elders of the village of Nazareth, he could have publicly divorced her and brought her to shame. In doing this, he could have also possibly kept the dowry paid to his family by Mary's family and demanded the return of the bride price he would have paid to Mary's family.

Joseph initially decided to "divorce her quietly." This would have preserved Mary from public shame but also meant great financial loss to himself and his family. He chose to cover her rather than expose her. He valued Mary as a human being over the financial structures of the *ketubah,* which would have benefited him if he divorced her. In this, we see how he was a *tzaddik*—generous and righteous.

After Joseph had decided to divorce Mary quietly, an angel appeared to him in a dream and told him something interesting.

READ MATTHEW 1:20. What does the angel tell Joseph?

Why does the angel tell Joseph not to be afraid? By marrying Mary even though she was pregnant, he would be putting himself in a position to share the cultural shame that would come from everyone who did not believe that she was visited by an angel, or that she was still a virgin. He would have been implicated in her prenuptial pregnancy. Not only did Joseph choose to stay with Mary and cover her shame, he entered into it with her. His decision to obey the angel meant sacrificing finances and reputation. His yes was costly. He risked and was rewarded with the honor and adventure of being Jesus's earthly father.

Sometimes, saying yes to the adventures the living God brings our way will be risky, costly, and will test us. I have a phrase handwritten on a sticky note on my bathroom mirror. As I write this, it has been there for seven years. I see it every morning and every evening. It is there to remind me of a simple yet powerful principle Joseph and Mary followed and one that I want to follow: *The reward is on the other side of obedience.*

> *The reward is on the other side of obedience.*

I have learned that sometimes the next things won't come until I take the step of obedience right in front of me. I have to step by faith and trust that the living God will take me by the hand and go on the adventure with me. He has not failed me yet. He did not fail Joseph or Mary. He will not fail you.

Take a moment to reflect on the adventures God has brought your way in the past. In what way did God meet you in your yes?

Is there an opportunity God is currently asking you to say a risky yes to? What is the next step of obedience for you? How can you make plans today to take that next step?

✱ Church of the Nativity, Bethlehem, Israel

SNAPSHOT 2

A Portrait of Mary

Now that we have the historical and cultural context of Luke (Session One), and have studied Matthew's birth narrative through the eyes of Joseph in Matthew, we are ready to look at the incarnation through the eyes of Mary in Luke.

In his Gospel, Luke quotes from the book of Isaiah more than any other biblical book. He reaches back to many of the prophet's words to help explain what Jesus was doing during His life and ministry. For Luke, Jesus is understood best through the prophetic ministry of Isaiah. As we move forward we will often feast on passages from Isaiah and Luke together to gain a deeper appreciation of Jesus in His first-century Jewish world, including His birth.

READ LUKE 1:26-38. What do we know about Mary from this passage?

Have you ever wondered what caused the living God to choose Mary as the mother of Jesus? Why her? What did she embody that caused the God of all creation to select her to carry, birth, and raise Jesus, the very Son of God? We certainly don't know the full mind of God here, but I think one verse gives us great insight into Mary and how it is that she will forever hold the honor of being Jesus's earthly mother.

> "I am the Lord's servant," Mary answered. "May your word to me be fulfilled."
> **LUKE 1:38a**

Mary's yes to the angel Gabriel was one of the hardest and riskiest yeses ever given to the living God in the whole story of the Bible. In Mary's world, girls were betrothed a year in advance of the actual marriage ceremony.[8] At the time, it was thought that a girl was "grown up" at twelve-and-a-half, and it was seen as a problem for her to be grown up and unmarried. Being unmarried at twelve-and-a-half was considered LATE.[9] So, Mary was probably eleven or twelve and premenstrual at the time of her betrothal to Joseph. In a culture where women found to be pregnant outside of marriage were sometimes stoned to death (honor killing), Mary said yes to the adventure of a lifetime. Whereas Joseph was described as a generous and righteous man, we can see that Mary was a young girl with great *gevurah*—the Hebrew word for courage and strength.[10]

✱ Wealthy Sepphoris mosaics *[top two images]* contrasted against nearby Nazareth *[bottom]*

Mary and her family lived in the northern Galilee region in a small village called Nazareth. Historically, Nazareth probably held a population of a few hundred people. It was a blip on the screen, a bump in the road. To the world, it would have felt insignificant in every way. Nazareth was overshadowed by a large, wealthy, Greco-Roman city called Sepphoris about three to five miles away. Sepphoris had temples, theaters, and brothels and was known as the jewel of the Galilee.[11]

In the first century, Galilee had quite the Gentile presence. Romans utilized Capernaum on the Sea of Galilee as a tax post along the International Trade Highway that ran through the land. Thus, the Jewish people of Galilee felt the oppressive Roman presence in many ways. It was a place of bloodshed, violence, political turmoil, and Roman aggression at will. Some seven hundred years before the birth of Jesus, Isaiah prophesied about this region of darkness and the light that would break forth into their gloom.

> Nevertheless, there will be no more gloom for those who were in distress. In the past he humbled the land of Zebulun (Nazareth) and the land of Naphtali (Capernaum), but in the future he will honor Galilee of the nations [Gentiles], by the way of the Sea, beyond the Jordan.
>
> **ISAIAH 9:1**

Remember, Caesar's *Pax Romana* or Roman peace was established and maintained through bloodshed and imperial pressure. Rome was oppressive, even to the point of killing whomever and whatever got in the way of her total dominance. Mary knew that the birth of her son would initiate a new kingdom, a new rule and reign—a rule of justice and righteousness, a rule of peace made available to all people in a tired and wearied world. Jesus's birth signaled the beginning of an overthrow. Kingdom was coming into a world of empire.

The peace Jesus ushered into the world also came through bloodshed—His own, as the sacrificial Lamb of God on the cross. His death won life for all who believe—life now, and eternal life forever. The way of the Caesars will one day cease, and when the kingdom of God is fully realized, there will be no end to the rule and reign of Jesus.

READ LUKE 1:46-55. This is often referred to as Mary's Magnificat.

Songs have always been an integral and important part of defining the history and culture of people groups. Andrew Fletcher once wrote, "Let me make the songs of a nation, and I care not who makes its laws."[12] Several songs in Scripture were penned by women.

Look up the passages below and complete the chart. You may have to skim the verses before the song to find the occasion for each.

Passage	Who sang?	Occasion for song?
EXODUS 15:21		
JUDGES 5		
1 SAMUEL 2:1-10		

Which of these verses of adoration stands out to you today? Why?

As we've just read, Mary also contributed to this rich, feminine history of biblical songs. Mary's song is deeply rooted in the knowledge that the Son in her belly would reorder the world and usher in peace. Those on high would be brought down low. Those who were low would be raised up.

LOOK AGAIN AT ISAIAH 9:1.

Why would there be no more gloom? How would Galilee be honored? It would become the cradle of the Messiah born into the earth—the beginning of the fulfillment of the end of Isaiah 9.

READ ISAIAH 9:6. **What characteristics of God are highlighted in both this verse and in Mary's Magnificat?**

Mary could feel the prophetic promise of Isaiah 9 growing inside her for nine months. She risked greatly by participating in this grand prophecy coming true through her literal body. She risked the potential of not being believed in her story of Gabriel's visit and news. She risked her reputation, as some would always believe that Jesus was illegitimate; she was willing to carry that stigma throughout her life. This miraculous, virgin birth plan was not safe for her in her world. But she wanted to see Scripture fulfilled in her day and time, in her life, and because of this she is honored as Jesus's earthly mother for all time.

Write your own short magnificat for something God has done, or is doing, in your life.

SNAPSHOT 3

The Shepherds

READ LUKE 2:8-20.

Our third snapshot in this session's theme of incarnation is the continued birth story of Jesus with the angelic visit and *euangelion* (good news) given to shepherds near Bethlehem.[13] In the world of Caesar Augustus and the Roman Empire, the living God kept reaching out to those on the margins and outskirts of society to invite them into and include them in the grand story of Jesus's birth. The Spirit kept moving away from the centers of power toward the powerless, centralizing them in the incarnational story.

We are learning that the living God not only sees those on the margins, but He also calls them to actively engage and partner with Him in the divine work of kingdom moving into empire. In Luke 1–2, He had already come to a common priest (Zechariah), an older barren woman (Elizabeth), and two peasant-poor inhabitants of Nazareth (Joseph and Mary). The movement outward continued with the angels' visit to the shepherds.

READ LUKE 2:8-15. **Why do you think the angel declared the good news of the Savior to the shepherds?**

From a gospel perspective, if you are on the outskirts, you are in a perfect position to be found and brought into the plan of God for the world. Those who suffer know how to comfort. Those who suffer know the importance of compassion, both giving it and receiving it. Caesar's *euangelion* was only good for those on top. The *euangelion* proclaimed by the angels to the shepherds was "good news that will cause great joy for all the people" (Luke 2:10b).

Historically and culturally, shepherds were considered dirty, even dangerous. They carried the reputation of being given to thievery and dishonesty. Even worse, the rich often treated them as invisible.[14] But what we see in Scripture is that the invisible ones in Jesus's day would become the visible and audible heralds and witnesses of the true *euangelion* of Jesus's birth.

Long before the first-century world of Jesus, the Egyptians thought of Joseph's family and livestock as detestable (Old Testament Joseph, not Jesus's earthly father; Gen. 46:31-34). They would settle Joseph's nomadic, shepherding family in the region of Goshen, far away from the settled and sophisticated centers of Egyptian culture and power. We see a much larger biblical theme emerging here—pharaoh versus shepherd. Powerful versus powerless. Empire versus kingdom. Caesar Augustus of Rome and Jesus of Nazareth.

It is important to note here that so many of the greats of Israel were shepherds—Abraham, Isaac, Jacob, Rachel, Moses, Aaron, David, Amos, and others. Among those, only David ever sat on a throne. They walked with the living God and their flocks through Goshen, Sinai, and Canaan. And in John 10, Jesus described Himself as the "good shepherd," a Shepherd who would lay His life down for His flock.

Knowing the reputation shepherds had at the time, why do you think Jesus identified Himself as a good shepherd?

In this depiction of himself, Jesus was identifying with those on the margins—the invisibles in his first-century Jewish world. Through the imagery of shepherding, Jesus identified Himself not only with what shepherds did in tending sheep but also with who they were as a marginalized group in society. Jesus's earthly parents likely recounted to Him the story of His birth, and God's inclusion of shepherds among those first to hear of the Messiah's arrival was certainly a detail Jesus would have known.

READ LUKE 2:8 AGAIN.

Many of us have read these words each and every Christmas season. They have likely become deeply familiar to us. While I was studying in Israel in 2007, we were sitting in a field outside Bethlehem, reading and unpacking this shepherd-passage while anchored in its historical and cultural world. As we were studying, something emerged—a possible understanding of something unique about these shepherds who were visited by an angelic host. It's often referred to as *Migdal Eder.*

Migdal Eder means "tower of the flock" and was first mentioned in Genesis 35:21 as a tower near Ephrath (Bethlehem). Rachel, one of Jacob's wives, died during a road trip after giving birth and was buried near Bethlehem and *Migdal Eder* (Gen. 35:16-21). It shows up again through the prophet Micah in 4:8 and 5:2 as the prophetic place where a ruler would emerge—a "ruler over Israel, whose origins are from of old, from ancient times" (5:2). This would come to be seen as a messianic prophecy by many in the Christian church.[15]

The church historian Eusebius connected the fields that these shepherds were in while watching their flocks at night with *Migdal Eder*, most likely located between Jerusalem and Bethlehem (just miles apart).[16] The angelic announcement to these shepherds was the first true *euangelion*—the good news of Jesus the Messiah incarnated into the world.

The sacrificial system within the temple in Jerusalem remained until Titus and the Romans destroyed the city and Temple in AD 70. The sacrificial system ended at that time.[17]

Both the Mishnah and the Talmudic writings mention a consecrated area between Jerusalem and Bethlehem with special, consecrated animals that were only used for sacrifice in the temple in Jerusalem. Thus, there is a possibility that the shepherds in the birth story of Jesus were temple precinct shepherds, specially tasked with shepherding sheep who would be sacrificed, many during Passover.

READ EXODUS 12:1-8,21-28. What were the instructions regarding the Passover lamb?

How were the people to answer the question of what the ceremony meant to them?

While we do not know for sure if the shepherds of Luke 2 were temple shepherds shepherding temple sheep near *Migdal Eder*, who better to announce the birth of the "Lamb of God, who takes away the sin of the world" (John 1:29) than the very ones shepherding the current sheep within the sacrificial system?

One of the most beautiful things about Joseph, Mary, and Joseph's family was that they welcomed the shepherds in when they arrived to see the newly born Messiah. They extended ancient Near Eastern hospitality to those on the social outskirts. After seeing Jesus for themselves, the shepherds held the honor of being the first announcers of the true *euangelion*.

> So they hurried off and found Mary and Joseph, and the baby, who was lying in a manger. When they had seen him, they spread the word concerning what had been told them about this child, and all who heard it were amazed at what the shepherds said to them.
> **LUKE 2:16-18**

Why do you think people were amazed at what the shepherds said to them?

In what ways is the *euangelion* of Jesus still amazing to us today?

✱ Stone manger

More about:
EUANGELION

The word ***euangelion*** is Greek for good news. It's where we get words like evangelism. Adding *eu* to the front of a Greek word is a way of making the term positive. The meaning of *eu* is "good." For example, the English term *eulogy* combines *eu* and the Greek term for "word," *logos*. To give a eulogy is to give a "good word." The term *euangelion* is also the combination of two Greek words: *eu* and *angelion*, meaning "message." The meaning of the gospel, therefore, is "good message."[18]

SNAPSHOT 4

Tikvah

✱ A country road in the Judean mountains near Jerusalem

Our focus this session has been the incarnation, which means "to take on flesh." The living God of all creation took on flesh and came to earth as a baby, virgin-born to two Jewish parents. The true Son of God broke into human history, and His birth brought the dawn of the kingdom of God moving into empire. When I take teams to Israel, we sit in a model of a first-century Jewish home in the Bethlehem area, and I teach through Luke 2. Sitting in that ancient home, feasting on Luke 2, I always feel something—*hope*.

What comes to your mind when you read the word *hope*? What feelings, situations, people, or places spring into your thoughts?

Hope is my word for this year. It's a lovely word. We love this word. We want more of it in our lives. We want to be hopeful people. We want to give hope to others. But what exactly is biblical hope? The Hebrew word for hope is *tikvah*. It means "hope, cord, expectation."[19] It is active, not passive. Hope cords us; it tethers us to the living God and to each other in this world. We feel hopeless when we feel disconnected, "uncorded," isolated, or alone. We feel hopeful when we are corded, when we feel connected to God and others in meaningful ways.

About a year ago I met a young woman named Eh Lay Wah. She lives in Nashville, Tennessee, but she is originally from Myanmar. She was going through my *Jesus and Women* Bible study, and a friend of mine introduced us. As she learned about Jesus's ministry of justice and righteousness, she started growing in her understanding of God's love for her as a woman in this world.

Months after meeting her, Eh Lay Wah reached out to me because her pastor asked her to teach on the birth of Jesus (Luke 2) for a special Christmas service at her church. He had noticed a transformational change in her. She was walking in the justice and righteousness given to her by Jesus as He generously lifted her up.

She asked if we could meet and work on her teaching together because she was nervous. My heart almost burst out of my chest! I was so excited to share in this adventure with her. We met at a coffee shop a few times and sat in the birth story of Jesus together. It was absolutely amazing.

I was able to attend that special Christmas service and support Eh Lay Wah as she shared in her native language of Burmese. I did not understand many of the words, but I felt the living, hopeful story of Jesus's birth pouring out of her mouth as she shared Luke 2 with her people. It was one of my most favorite moments of 2022. Eh Lay Wah took hope in her hands and blessed her whole church.

Sitting there, listening to the birth story of Jesus in a church service, I felt that same feeling I feel when teaching Luke 2 in an ancient home in the Bethlehem region—*hope*.

The birth of Jesus did not happen in a vacuum, but in a long lineage and history of generations. Both Matthew and Luke provide a genealogy of Jesus's family line. And in order to learn more about biblical hope, we now look to a woman within that genealogy to show us the way.

We find the story of this woman who acted with hope in Joshua 2. Rahab was a Canaanite prostitute living in the city of Jericho. The Israelites were about to take the city, and two Israelite spies went into Jericho and interacted with Rahab. She hid the spies from the men in her city.

READ JOSHUA 2:8-13. **What reason did Rahab give for her heroic, life-saving actions? What did she ask in return?**

The spies promised her that if she would hold a scarlet cord out of her window, they would spare her and her family when they conquered the city. Rahab acted with expectation.

The word used in this story for "cord" is *tikvah*.[20] Rahab took hope in her hands and held that scarlet cord out of her window. She held out hope, and it saved her and her entire family. Biblical hope isn't an emotion we passively carry around in our hearts—*Well, I sure hope it works out*. No. Biblical hope is something we actively carry in our hands. We are hopeful when we act, move, and partner with the living God in bringing *shalom* and salvation into the world.

What would *tikvah*, biblical hope, look like in your life or in a current situation?

Rahab went on to be the mother of Boaz who would become the great-grandfather of King David after serving as the kinsman redeemer for Ruth (Ruth 4:13-17). A Moabite woman, widowed and far from home, Ruth was in a vulnerable position before meeting Boaz. Much like her then-future mother-in-law, Ruth acted on hope. She made a declaration of faithfulness to Naomi (the mother of her former husband) and worked in the fields to provide food for them both. Boaz saw her working in his fields and eventually took her as his wife, perhaps because of his Canaanite mother. He may have witnessed, or at least heard stories of, what it looks like to take hope in your hands. Rahab's hope saved her and her whole family.

TURN TO MATTHEW 1. READ VERSES 5-6. **Draw out this branch of Jesus's family tree below.**

Generations are impacted when a woman lives with hope in her hands.

Jesus is our living hope. Let's cord ourselves to Him. Let's be women who take hope in our hands and live forward with active expectation and engagement in the kingdom of God moving into empire.

In the same region, shepherds were staying out in the fields and keeping watch at night over their flock.
Luke 2: 8

WATCH AND DISCUSS

WATCH THE SESSION TWO VIDEO. **Use the space below to take notes. Discuss the questions on the following page with your Bible study group. A more extensive leader guide is available for free download at lifeway.com/lukeintheland.**

To access the video sessions, use the instructions in the back of your Bible study book.

1. What is a risky yes you've said in the past? It can be silly or serious!

2. Read Luke 2:8-15 together. Why do you think the angel declared the good news of the Savior to the shepherds first? What does that tell you about the living God?

3. What came to your mind as you studied *tikvah*—biblical hope? Are there people or circumstances in your life that demonstrate that hope to you?

4. You wrote a magnificat during Snapshot 2. Read a couple (or all of them) out loud as a prayer to end your time together.

Session Three

INAUGURATION

SNAPSHOT 1

Jesus's Baptism in the Jordan River

Our focus for Session Three will be inauguration, which means the beginning, or genesis, of something. Jesus, the true Savior of the world, (not Caesar) grew up to serve and live as a Galilean Rabbi and sage of Israel. In the first-century Jewish world, age thirty was the age of rabbinic authority.[1] It makes perfect sense then when Luke tells us Jesus was thirty years old when He began His rabbinic ministry (Luke 3:23).

What was the historical, cultural marker of the beginning of Jesus's ministry as a Rabbi? In that world, you wouldn't just wake up one day and just declare yourself to be a rabbi. As we will see over and over again, the prophet Isaiah is the beginning of our understanding of Jesus's inauguration into rabbinic ministry.

READ ISAIAH 40:3-5.

The voice of one calling in the desert as a forerunner to the Messiah would be John the Baptist. His birth story is told in Luke 1 when the Lord opened the womb of barren Elizabeth. His father was Zechariah, the levitical priest who was serving in the temple when an angel appeared to him and told him he would have a son named John.

READ LUKE 1:13-17. **How did the angel describe what John's future would be like?**

How would John fulfill Isaiah 40:3-5?

What Old Testament figure did the angel compare John to?

In Matthew 3, John is described as wearing clothes "made of camel's hair, and he had a leather belt around his waist" (v. 4). In 2 Kings 1:8, Elijah is described as wearing something very similar: "a garment of hair and had a leather belt around his waist." The Bible rarely describes what people looked like, so we should pay attention here. John was compared to Elijah throughout Scripture and not only because they wore similar clothes. Elijah was revered as one of the greatest and most powerful prophets in Israel's history.

Why do you think John is compared to Elijah in Scripture? IF YOU NEED SOME HINTS, LOOK UP A COUPLE OF THE FOLLOWING PASSAGES: 1 KINGS 18:30-34; ISAIAH 40:3; MALACHI 4:5; MATTHEW 17:10-13; JOHN 1:15-23.

In Luke 3, John the Baptist emerged from the wilderness in the region near the Jordan River, looking like Elijah, operating in power like Elijah, and calling the people to a "baptism of repentance for the forgiveness of sins" (v. 3). Many followed him and underwent this baptism.

Baptism in John and Jesus's first-century Jewish world was diverse and varied; people were often baptized for different reasons. At the time, the five main reasons for baptism were:

1. **Ritual purification**—Leviticus 13–14; Numbers 19;

2. **Proselytes**—converting to Judaism;

3. **Priests and kings**—consecration to religious or political authority;

4. **Doctrinal identification**—John's "baptism of repentance";

5. **Submission to rabbinic authority**—baptized into a rabbi's name/yoke.[2]

So, what was the reason for Jesus's baptism in the Jordan River with John the Baptist present? It was His inauguration into rabbinic ministry (similar to number three above). Jesus's baptism served as His ordination, consecration, and inauguration as a Rabbi of Israel, with John the Baptist and the people present serving as His witnesses.

After forty days and nights in the wilderness, Jesus began traveling around the Galilee in the power of the Spirit, teaching in the synagogues, proclaiming the kingdom of heaven, healing the sick, and casting out demons (Luke 4). Jesus emerged from the waters of His baptism and His time in the wilderness prepared to enter into His public ministry as a Rabbi.

If you've been baptized, think back to your baptism. What do you remember from that day?

If you haven't been baptized, what does baptism look like in the church you attend?

More about:
THE IMPORTANCE OF WITNESSES

Deuteronomy 17:6

Deuteronomy 19:15

Matthew 18:16

2 Corinthians 13:1

1 Timothy 5:19

Hebrews 10:28

1 John 5:8

I was baptized when I was nine years old. I remember it like it was yesterday. I remember my parents sitting on the front row of our local church. I remember my pastor baptizing me. My body can still remember the feeling of the waters as I went down and back up again. The people present bore witness to my baptism, promising to be a community that would love me and train me up as a young follower of Jesus.

Who was present at your baptism?

In the Bible, we often read of the importance of two or three witnesses in matters of discipline and legality. Having two to three witnesses legitimized an occasion.

The reality and involvement of the Trinity were beautifully evident at Jesus's baptism. The Father was audibly present while the Holy Spirit appeared in the form of a dove. Luke recorded God the Father as declaring from heaven:

> You are my Son, whom I love;
> with you I am well pleased.
>
> **LUKE 3:22b**

For the people present, sacred Scriptures would have flooded their minds as they heard these divine words from Jesus's heavenly Father. The Hebrew Bible (Old Testament) is composed of three sections—Torah (first five books), Nevi'im (prophets), and Ketuvim (the Writings—think Psalms, Proverbs, Song of Solomon, etc.). Here, in this moment of inauguration, the living God quotes from all three sections of the Hebrew Bible in affirming His Son Jesus:

- You are my Son—Psalm 2:7
- Whom I love—Genesis 22:2
- With you I am well pleased—Isaiah 42:1

Lastly, from a historic and cultural perspective, the location of Jesus's baptism held significance. Why was Jesus baptized in the Jordan River, in the region of the Judean wilderness? It was a hint back to previous stories and moments in Israel's history. This was known as the region of transferring authority. Moses passed the baton to Joshua here. Elijah passed the baton to Elisha here. And it was the place where John the Baptist symbolically passed the baton to Jesus. The forerunner, John, pointed everyone to Jesus—the Messiah, One greater than Moses, Joshua, Elijah, Elisha, and John the Baptist.

> The people were waiting expectantly and were all wondering in their hearts if John might possibly be the Messiah. John answered them all, "I baptize you with water. But one who is more powerful than I will come, the straps of whose sandals I am not worthy to untie. He will baptize you with the Holy Spirit and fire."
> **LUKE 3:15-16**

Who in your life has pointed you to Jesus? Tell about some of the ways they have been voices calling in the wilderness for you.

* Desert between Jerusalem and Jericho

SNAPSHOT 2

Davar in the Midbar

As we continue Luke's storyline in Luke 4, we might expect the next snapshot to be Jesus emerging from the Jordan River, freshly inaugurated as a Rabbi and heading straight to the synagogues, preaching and teaching, healing and casting out impure spirits. But, the Spirit of God had a different plan. As we will see, rather than moving toward ministry, Jesus was led away from ministry.

When reading with our Western eyes, one of the most interesting and unexpected verses in the entire Gospel of Luke is Luke 4:1.

> Jesus, full of the Holy Spirit, left the Jordan
> and was led by the Spirit into the wilderness.

Why the wilderness? The answer becomes clearer to us when we understand this passage in its historical, Jewish context.

We've all had wilderness experiences in life. Tell about one of your wilderness seasons.

When we wake up in a wilderness, our first question is usually, *How do I get out of this wilderness?* But the Jewish people asked a different question. Their first question was, *What is my* davar *in the* midbar*?*

The Hebrew word for *word* is *davar*. The Hebrew word for *wilderness* is *midbar*. These words share the same root word. Throughout the story of the Bible, we see God's people receiving His words while in the wilderness. We see that they received their *davar bamidbar*—their word in the wilderness.[3]

Glance over the chapters below and fill in the blanks on the chart.

Scripture	Who was in the wilderness?	What did they receive?
Exodus 3		
Exodus 20		*Gift of the Torah and Law*
1 Kings 19		
Galatians 1:17-18		*Prepared for apostolic ministry*

These biblical accounts can help us understand why the Spirit of God led Jesus into the wilderness immediately following His baptism and inauguration into rabbinic ministry and why the Jewish people would expect to receive a word in the wilderness. When I think about this, I imagine Jesus, full of the Holy Spirit, walking into the wilderness with His ears wide open to hear, expectant to inherit His *davar bamidbar*, His word in the wilderness.

Did you emerge from any of your wilderness seasons with a *davar*? How did God demonstrate His character to you in that season?

Matthew's Gospel moves into the Sermon on the Mount after Jesus's forty days and nights in the wilderness. Could it be that Jesus received His central teaching and *halakha* (way, path) during that time in the wilderness?[4] Both Matthew and Luke tell us that Jesus was tempted by the devil during His time in the wilderness.

READ LUKE 4:1-13. How did Jesus respond to each temptation from the devil?

Three temptations. Three responses given by Jesus through quoting Scripture. The word was with Jesus in the wilderness.

What were the three temptations? Are we still tempted in similar ways today?

What can we learn from the way Jesus overcame temptation? How can we apply His strategy in our own lives?

Think about one temptation you struggle to overcome. Use a concordance or search online to find some verses in Scripture that speak to your frequent temptation. Challenge yourself to write those verses in places you're often tempted, or to memorize them. This is a way you can always have Scripture at the ready to resist temptation. I've written a couple references to get you started.

- ☐ **2 Corinthians 10:5**
- ☐ **Philippians 4:8**
- ☐
- ☐
- ☐
- ☐

Numbers throughout the Bible often communicate important insights into the stories being told. The number forty is an interesting number we see over and over. In essence, when we see forty, we can know that signifies we should look for change.[5]

Let's string a few more biblical pearls together:

1. The flood lasted forty days and nights (Gen. 6).

2. The twelve Israelite spies' journey into the promised land was forty days (Num. 13:25).

3. The Israelites waited in the desert for forty years (Numbers).

4. Goliath taunted the Israelites in the Valley of Elah for forty days when David showed up (1 Sam. 17:16).

5. Saul, David, and Solomon all ruled for forty-ish years.

So, we pay attention to what Luke is trying to tell us when he mentions that Jesus was in the wilderness for forty days and forty nights. Look for change! Jesus emerged from the wilderness with His word (*davar*) and immediately started teaching in the synagogues around the Galilee. In other words, His ministry was ON! Kingdom was moving into empire, and the world would never be the same.

The Bible encourages us to reframe our Western sense of the wilderness. *Midbar* seasons are word seasons for us in our lives. Rather than running from the wilderness, we begin to settle in and tune our ears to hear. We posture ourselves in case the Lord has a *davar* for us in our *midbar*. The wilderness isn't the place of sheer endurance. It's the place of divine revelation, relationship, and inheritance of the word of the Lord.

In 2016, the Spirit of God led me into a wilderness season. I took a leap and resigned from the church where I had served for seventeen years. I knew I was supposed to resign, but I was afraid because I didn't know what was next. I love a plan and a paycheck, and I had neither. It felt like a significant faith jump, and I walked into the unknown on June 30, 2016. I felt my feet walking into the wilderness.

Right after resigning, I planned a trip with some friends to go visit a friend in Pittsburgh, Pennsylvania. I sat down on the plane, put my tray table down and set my Bible on it. I was struggling. In all honesty, I was afraid, unsure, unsteady, and pretty much freaked out. I remember praying—lamenting to the living God that He had led me into a wilderness. How would I survive? How would I pay my bills?

In that moment on the plane, I didn't even know what to read; I just knew I needed the comfort of my Bible. I don't necessarily recommend this method of Bible study as a regular practice, but the living God met me in my desperation. I literally opened it up, put my finger aimlessly down on the page, and here's what I read:

> Can God really spread a table
> in the wilderness?
> **PSALM 78:19b**

The very language I had been giving to the Lord in prayer was the language of Scripture that met me on that airplane. I sat there stunned. Psalm 78:19 became my *davar bamidbar*—my word in my wilderness. I meditated on it often. I wrote it on a sticky note on my bathroom mirror, and I recited it to myself as I drove around my city, visited with my friends, and on my walks with my dog, Chester. That verse held me, supported me, and anchored me in hopeful expectation.

As I write this today, it has been almost seven years since that moment on the airplane. I can tell you that the living God can indeed prepare a table in the wilderness. He met my needs the whole way and gave me my very own *davar bamidbar.* I see the wilderness differently now. It's a place of deep and rich transformation, growth, and maturity. It's the place where the word of the Lord finds us.

✱ Desert between Jerusalem and Jericho

3 SNAPSHOT

✱ Ruins of the synagogue at Capernaum

Jesus in the Synagogue at Nazareth

READ LUKE 4:14-15.

So far, we have witnessed Jesus's baptism in the Jordan River—His inauguration into rabbinic ministry. We have also witnessed Jesus spending forty days and nights in the *midbar*, perhaps emerging with His *davar bamidbar*—His word in the wilderness. Luke continues his brilliant storytelling in Luke 4 with the beginning of Jesus's public ministry.

READ LUKE 4:14-15. **Where was Jesus teaching? What were the people's reactions to His teaching?**

Kingdom was now moving into empire and a better king than Caesar was on the move. The true *soter* (Savior) of the world had been born in Bethlehem, was raised in Nazareth, and was now beginning His ministry of inaugurating the kingdom of God—reversing the curse and making all things new. Salvation had come in the person of Jesus and was moving toward people—rich people, poor people, Jews and Gentiles, men and women. Jesus came for everyone, as we will see over and over throughout Luke's Gospel. Who did Jesus come for? E'erybody!

Throughout Luke's Gospel, Jesus's two primary places of ministry were the synagogue and the table (table fellowship). Luke portrays Jesus as a Rabbi centered in preaching and eating—being with and among the people He came to save. The first synagogue service we see Jesus teach as a Rabbi in the book of Luke is in His hometown of Nazareth.

READ LUKE 4:16-22.

Participation in synagogue on the Sabbath was part of Jesus's life and custom (Luke 4:16). In the first century, synagogue was a place of community assembly—reading and hearing the Torah with robust discussion and debate about how to live out the text in everyday life. Judaism practiced a fixed calendar of readings from the Torah (the Law) and the Prophets throughout the synagogues.

Those gathered for worship physically stood during the reading of Scripture in respect and recognition of its authority. Then, they sat down for the rabbi's teaching. Rabbis would stand to read the Word and sit for their own teaching to indicate their authority came under the supreme authority of Scripture.[6] Details in Matthew 5:1-2 before Jesus's teaching in the Sermon on the Mount provide a glimpse of these symbolic gestures.

While visiting the synagogue in His hometown of Nazareth, Jesus was tasked with reading from the Isaiah scroll. All those gathered, including Jesus, were likely aware of the fixed passage for the day. There might have been extra buzz and excitement on this *Shabbat* (Sabbath) because Isaiah 61 was a famous messianic passage with great significance for the Jewish people! They knew the prophesied Messiah would embody and fulfill Isaiah 61.

After reading these beautiful words from Isaiah, Jesus sat down. I imagine a hush coming across the assembly hall. Everyone wanted to hear Jesus's sermon (*deresha*) on this messianic passage.[7] As Jesus sat in His hometown synagogue of Nazareth, he spoke His first recorded words in the Gospel of Luke. In response to this famous messianic passage, pregnant with expectation, He said, "Today this scripture is fulfilled in your hearing" (Luke 4:21).

In that moment, Jesus made a public claim to be the long-awaited Messiah.

How did the people in the synagogue respond to this?

At first, those in the Nazarene synagogue marveled and spoke well of Jesus, seemingly embracing His claim of being Messiah. This is a really interesting response. How would you have responded if someone from your home church, whom you had known your whole life, had claimed to be the Messiah?

Here's a historical and cultural note on the name of this first-century village—Nazareth. The word might have come from the Hebrew word *netzer* meaning "branch" or "offshoot."[8] It is possible that the people of Nazareth would have connected this with Isaiah 11:1, "A shoot will come from the stump of Jesse: from his roots a Branch will bear fruit." The people of Nazareth might have viewed themselves as these "shoots" or "branches" and could have lived with a village-wide expectation that the Messiah would come from among them. If that is true, it would have made sense to them that the Messiah would rise up from among them.

According to Luke, everything was going well so far during Jesus's first recorded synagogue service. But Jesus wasn't done talking, and the people weren't done responding to Him.

READ LUKE 4:23-30. In your own words, what was Jesus saying to the people in His hometown?

How did the people respond to this part of Jesus's teaching?

Jesus's synagogue service ended with Him almost being stoned to death. Everything was going so well at first. *What happened?* How did it go from everyone speaking well of Him to trying to stone Him?

Remember, Jesus's two central places of ministry were synagogue and table. Both were seen as exclusive; Jews went to their own synagogues and temples, while Romans, Greeks, and pagans worshiped in theirs. Meanwhile, table fellowship was one of the highest affiliations in the first-century world. Those whom you ate with, you welcomed, embraced, and accepted. Because of this, Jews did not readily associate with outside groups, such as Samaritans and pagans. They avoided entering the homes of Gentiles as they considered such spaces unclean.

The Jewish people in Nazareth were ready to accept a Messiah who had come to save the Jewish people. But their vision of Jesus's table and the kingdom of God was small and misguided. It did not include Gentiles.

Jesus, however, went on to include in His teaching two Gentiles who received miraculous healing and help from the Lord: the healing of the Sidonian widow in Zarephath through Elijah (1 Kings 17) and the healing of Naaman the Syrian through Elisha (2 Kings 5:1-19).

Jesus's vision of the kingdom of God was much wider than that of His Jewish audience—it included the nations. Jesus was coming for e'erybody, e'erwhere.

The "shoots" and "branches" (Nazarenes) "were furious when they heard this" (Luke 4:28). They took Jesus to a ridge outside of Nazareth and intended to stone Him. *The Mishnah* gives rules for stoning: the guilty person would be stoned naked; they would be thrown down from somewhere twice the height of the person; and if the fall didn't kill him or her, then each witness would throw one stone. If the person died, so be it. If the person lived, so be it.[9]

The fact Jesus was able to "walk right through the crowd and went on his way" (Luke 4:30) indicates that no one was willing to act as a judicial witness against Him in that moment. They were furious, but no one came forward willing to strip Him, throw Him down, or stone Him.

Luke's first recorded synagogue service of Jesus as a Rabbi of Israel and Messiah to the world was a doozy. Jesus read and taught famous Isaiah passages, He proclaimed to be the fulfillment of Isaiah 61, and by the end, the people expressed both amazement and fury. And we're only in Luke 4!

✱ Temple model

SNAPSHOT 4

✱ Capernaum synagogue site

Capernaum: Jesus's Second Hometown

Believe it or not, we are still not done with Luke 4. The storytelling continues as Jesus leaves Nazareth (the city of His upbringing) to go to Capernaum—His hometown and ministry base as an adult and Rabbi of Israel (Matt. 4:13).

Capernaum had great importance, primarily because of its location on the Sea of Galilee. The International Coastal Highway, a popular passageway for trade and commerce, linked three continents (Asia, Africa, and Europe) and went through Capernaum. Throughout history, nations warred over the land because they wanted to control this highway and regulate international trade via taxation. This explains why so many Romans were living in Capernaum in the first century. In Luke 7:1-10, we see Jesus interact with a Roman centurion in Capernaum.

For the Jews, Capernaum was home to a large synagogue with an accompanying *bet sefer* or "house of the book."[10] Synagogues in the first century often had a *bet sefer*, or house of learning, built onto them. Synagogue was a place of assembly, community, prayer, hearing Scripture, and discussing and debating it. The *bet sefer* was a place of study associated with the synagogue. Capernaum's house of learning was exceptional in the Galilee region in the first century. It's interesting to note that it was a Roman who financed the building of the synagogue in Capernaum.

When I take teams to Israel, we always visit Capernaum. The dark basalt ruins of the first-century synagogue that Jesus attended are still there to this day. A lighter-stoned fourth-century synagogue was built over it. I always enjoy taking teams into that Capernaum synagogue site and reading Luke 4:31-37—a biblical story that happened in that very place.

READ LUKE 4:31-44. Create a brief timeline of what happened in these verses. We don't know that this is the exact order of events—remember, we're seeing snapshots!—but we can learn from the sequence Luke outlines here.

The rest of Luke 4 gives us insight into a rhythm of ministry that Jesus practiced during His earthly ministry. It was a rhythm of engagement and rest. Jesus moved toward people for seasons and moments of ministry and then rested with moments of recovery, restoration, and renewal in prayer and solitude.

We see this rhythm play out in this snapshot in Luke 4. Luke tells us that a demon-possessed man attended the Capernaum synagogue on a day when Jesus was there. It has always been interesting to me that demon-possessed people went to synagogue. Darkness and light together in a synagogue. I would think they would shun synagogue and all the Scriptures, prayers, and beautiful, holy things happening during a synagogue service. But what we see in this snapshot is that Jesus called the demon out of the man, restoring him. Not a bad day at church!

From synagogue, Jesus went to Peter's mother-in-law's home and healed her of a fever. We often see this dual ministry of Jesus casting out demons and healing the sick. We see darkness being turned back on itself and health overriding sickness. Both of these were ways Jesus was ushering in the kingdom of God—the rule and reign of the living God in the earth as it is in heaven. Jesus was casting out darkness and bringing in light.

Every time I come to Luke 4:42, I breathe deep: "At daybreak, Jesus went out to a solitary place." After moments of preaching, casting out, and bringing in, He retreated into solitude. Healthy living as a follower of Jesus invites us to locate our own rhythms of engagement and rest. There's some kind of flow to life that aids us as we partner with the living God to bring the kingdom to the earth as it is in heaven.

Rest is actually part of the work. One of the things that has helped me greatly with this flow of engagement and rest is to schedule my rest days first and my work days second. The first things that get penciled into my calendar at the start of a new year are my rest days. Then, I schedule my work days around them. This has helped me cultivate a deeper appreciation for Sabbath and for the ministry of rest in my life. It also gives me the opportunity to be an agent of rest for others. I often ask people what their rest and recovery practices look like alongside their work practices.
I want to grow and mature into a balanced life and ministry of engagement and rest, and I hope to invite others into that as well.

How well do you rest?

What are some of your rest practices?

How are you honoring God with your rest?

What would it look like for you to schedule your rest days first?

How might that affect your work?

Jesus, full of the
Holy Spirit, left the
Jordan and was led
by the Spirit into
the wilderness.
Luke 4:1

WATCH AND DISCUSS

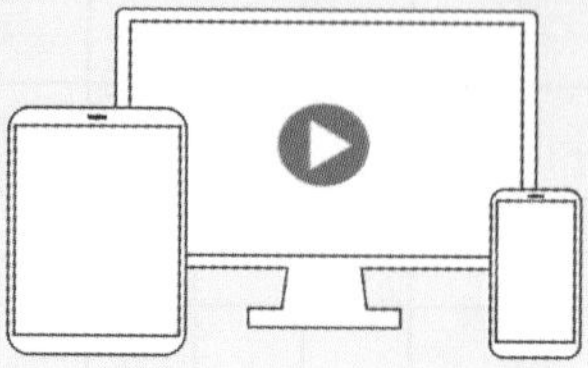

WATCH THE SESSION THREE VIDEO. **Use the space below to take notes. Discuss the questions on the following page with your Bible study group. A more extensive leader guide is available for free download at lifeway.com/lukeintheland.**

To access the video sessions, use the instructions in the back of your Bible study book.

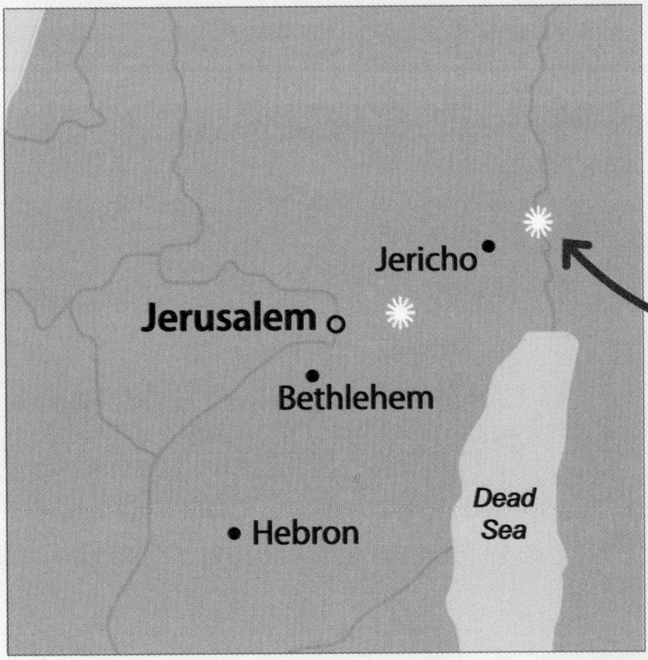

Jordan River & the wilderness

1. For those in the group who have been baptized, share stories from your baptisms. Help those in the group who have not been baptized to know what it looks like in your church and answer any questions they may have regarding baptism.

2. Have you ever received a devar bamidbar? Share about that experience. How did God demonstrate His character to you in that season?

3. Read Luke 4:16-22 together. What was Jesus saying about who He is and what His mission is in this teaching?

4. Is it difficult for you to rest? Share your answers about rest with the group, encouraging one another to find rest this week.

INVITATION

SNAPSHOT 1

Jesus Choosing & Inviting Disciples

Our snapshots for Session Four will be centered in invitation. The basic meaning of "invitation" is to request someone to go somewhere or to do something. Over and over this session we will feast on snapshots of Jesus inviting people to follow Him, walk with Him, minister with Him—to be His disciples. And we will be surprised and moved by some of the people He invited.

In Session Three, Luke told the stories of Jesus's baptism, wilderness experience, and the genesis of His rabbinic and messianic ministry in His hometowns of Nazareth and Capernaum. The kingdom of God was coming to earth through the life and ministry of Jesus. He could have done these things alone, but He chose to embody the kingdom and engage the world alongside His disciples.

Jesus lived out the fullness of invitation. He invited men and women to go somewhere and do something with Him—to bring heaven to earth, to bring the kingdom of God into the realms of empire, to begin working a profound restoration, renewal, and redemption. There is an ancient proverb that says, "If you want to go fast, go alone. If you want to go far, go together." The disciples who were chosen and invited by Jesus would carry the gospel of Jesus to the ends of the earth—and they would do it together.

READ LUKE 5:1-11. What can we know about Simon Peter, James, and John from this passage?

Among the first people Jesus formally invited to become His disciples were those who lived within His own region of Galilee. They worked on and around the Sea of Galilee.

The Sea of Galilee was known by other names:

Lake Tiberias – Tiberias was a city founded by Herod Antipas on the coast of the sea and named in honor of the Emperor Tiberias (Luke 3:1), the emperor of Rome during Jesus's earthly ministry.

✱ Capernaum

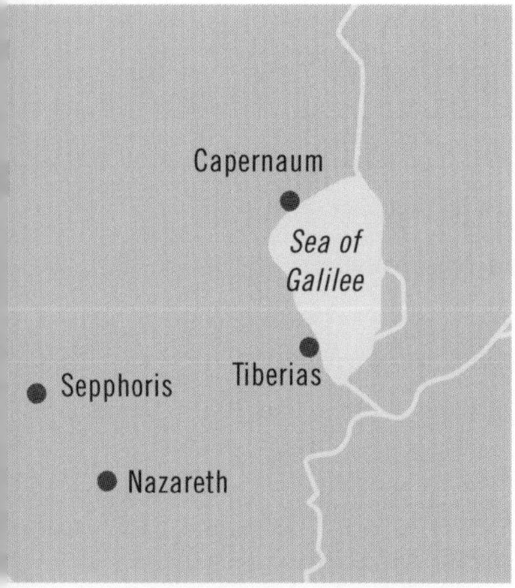

Lake Kinneret or Gennesaret – *Kinneret* means "harp" in Hebrew. It is sometimes called Lake Kinneret because the sea is shaped like a harp. The name Gennesaret (see Luke 5:1) comes from the same root word.[1]

Many things made Jesus unique as a Rabbi of Israel in the first-century Jewish world. Historically, Jesus wasn't the only one claiming to be the Messiah. He wasn't the only one performing miracles. He wasn't the only one who could heal people. He wasn't the only one who could cast out demons. Interestingly enough, these weren't necessarily the things that made Him unique, although they certainly made Him stand out.

Luke emphasized three things that made Jesus a profoundly unique Rabbi in His first-century Jewish world.

✱ Sculpture of the outline of the Sea of Galilee in Tiberias

1. JESUS PRACTICED TABLE FELLOWSHIP WITH UNLIKELY GUESTS.

He often ate with tax collectors and sinners, with the *am ha aretz* (people of the land).[2] Remember, table fellowship was vitally important in Jesus's world. Jesus, the great Rabbi, was welcoming, embracing, and accepting sinners at His table, affiliating with them and sharing meals with them.

Jesus earned a negative reputation among religious leaders for this table fellowship practice (Matt. 11:19). I smile every time I read Matthew 11:19, and I often ask myself the question: *How much was Jesus eating and drinking with tax collectors and sinners that He was called a "drunkard" and a "glutton"?* I imagine it was A LOT!

2. JESUS INCLUDED WOMEN AS HIS DISCIPLES.

In Luke 10, we see Mary sitting at Jesus's feet. This was a formal phrase, used for disciples of a rabbi. In this well-known story, Mary's sister, Martha, tells Jesus that she is worried about the work Mary is not helping her with. However, Jesus responds to her, saying, "you are worried and upset about many things" (v. 41). It may be that Mary was upset about more than shared meal responsibilities. Perhaps, her worries included her sister's position, sitting at Jesus's feet among the male disciples—an unusual scene around a rabbi at that time.

TURN TO LUKE 8:1-3. Who is listed by name here? What does it say they were doing?

In Luke 8, we will see a list of female *talmidim* (Hebrew for disciples) traveling in itinerant fashion with Jesus and the other disciples. Three are listed: Mary Magdalene, Joanna the wife of Chuza, and Susanna; and then we read the phrase "and many others" (vv. 1-3). We know these women were providing financial support along the way. However, if they were *only* providing financial support, they could have given their financial gifts and stayed home. Instead, they are present—traveling with Jesus and bearing witness to Him bringing heaven to earth, the kingdom of God to the ground.

3. JESUS CHOSE HIS DISCIPLES.

Jesus's culture was one in which people chose their rabbis. The lesser reached for the greater. *Rabbi* comes from the Hebrew root *rav,* which carries the meaning of "great, large or much."[3] To have the honor of being the disciple of a "great one" was a high honor indeed, one worth pursuing.

Jesus came on the scene and started doing the choosing. The greater was reaching for the lesser and inviting them to be His *talmidim* (disciples). This would be like Michael Jordan choosing you to play on the Chicago Bulls with him. Or Tiger Woods inviting you to play golf with him in a PGA championship tournament. Or the late Aretha Franklin hearing you sing and inviting you on tour to sing with her. The examples could go on and on.

More about:
FISHING IN THE SEA OF GALILEE

"Fishing was done along the shores, not out in the deep. Bethsaida, the coastal town, means 'house of fishing.' Some of the disciples were from that village. Fishermen not only were skilled in catching fish, but were also skilled in drying, smoking, pickling, and salting fish as most of the catch was shipped throughout the Roman empire.

Seine net fishing was the kind of fishing Jesus mentioned in Matthew 13:47-50. A large dragnet was weighed down so that the net hung vertically in the water. Then, a team would pull it to shore and fish would be sorted (kosher, non-kosher)."[5]

Can you imagine four, ordinary, common, Jewish fisherman; two sets of brothers—Peter and Andrew, James and John—living an average day in their fishermen lives when Jesus shows up, and chooses them to be four of His disciples? Jesus meets them right where they are. With beautiful, poetic language, he extends an invitation and a calling—"Don't be afraid; from now on you will fish for people" (Luke 5:10). A great *rav* of Israel was standing in front of them, choosing and inviting them to go somewhere and do something with Him. The greater was reaching for the lesser.

Their response was just as beautiful. How did they answer Jesus's invitation in Luke 5:11?

This snapshot reminds me of that great line in *The Last Battle* by C. S. Lewis: "We must go on and take the adventure that shall fall to us."[4] I have this quote on my refrigerator, and it has been there for years now. I see it every morning while my coffee is brewing. I want to be like the disciples in this snapshot. I want to go on and take the kingdom of God adventures that come to me. I want to wholeheartedly accept the invitation to go somewhere and do something with the living God in this world.

How Will We Recognize the Messiah?

SNAPSHOT 2

READ LUKE 5:12-16. Does anything in this snapshot story surprise you?

These five verses in the Gospel of Luke may not seem at first glance to be overly significant or unique compared to other snapshots in his Gospel, but this snapshot is massive in the messianic ministry of Jesus. It's a biggie. It's a snapshot to be reckoned with in the context of first-century Judaism and Jesus's rabbinic ministry within it. We will need to spend some time here, feasting slowly and unpacking this snapshot in its historical, cultural context.

Think about this. If you were living two thousand years ago in Galilee, Samaria, or Judea, how would you recognize the Messiah when He arrived? How would you know it was Him? He wouldn't be ten feet tall, glowing like a light bulb, speaking with a voice like thunder, and so forth. So, what were the Jewish people looking for in the first century when they were looking for the Messiah? When He came, how would they recognize Him?

As already mentioned, Jesus wasn't the only person performing miracles in the first-century world of the Jews. Honi the Circle Maker was known for drawing circles, standing in them, and praying for rain. And rain often came. He lived in the first century.[6] Rabbi Hanina ben Dosa was known for being able to heal the sick.[7]

He too lived in the first century. The Bible also gives us a glimpse into the fact that other Pharisees and their students could successfully perform exorcisms, driving and casting out demons (Matt. 12:22-28, emphasis on v. 27).

However, there were certain miracles that rabbis and religious leaders couldn't perform. There were certain healings they didn't possess the power to perform. And it was these miracles and healings that the people started associating with messianic presence and power. In other words, Messiah would be able to perform these miracles and healings, and they would differentiate Him from others claiming to be the messiah and those with miraculous ministries.

According to Dr. Ron Moseley, a scholar in Jewish studies and second temple history, there were four such miracles considered to be "messianic" in the first-century mindset of the people.[8] Did Jesus perform all four miracles during His rabbinic ministry? Yes. In this, He was demonstrating to the people that He was the Messiah by using miracles they were looking for as signposts for recognizing the Messiah when He arrived. Jesus met them right where they were in their messianic expectations. In demonstrating that He was the Messiah, He was inviting them to put their faith in Him and to faithfully walk with Him.

One of the four miracles was the ability to heal leprosy. Leprosy was, and is, a bacterial disease that affected the skin, eyes, nose, and nerves. Sometimes leprosy was used as a catch-all term for skin diseases in the Bible.[9] Leprosy was seen as the finger of God. Miriam, Moses's sister, was leprous, but the Lord healed her (Num. 12:10-15). The only other leprous healing story in the Old Testament was Naaman, a Gentile (2 Kings 5:1-14). The incredible rareness of leprosy being healed was mentioned by Jesus Himself in Luke 4:27 during His conversation at the Nazareth synagogue.

Leprosy was such a big deal that the Torah devotes two chapters to it in Leviticus 13 and 14. Any person with a supposed healing from leprosy was to go to the priest. A detailed description of what needed to happen is outlined as follows:

1. The priest had to establish that the person actually had been afflicted with leprosy.

2. The priest had to establish that the person had indeed been healed from leprosy.

3. The priest had to establish who had performed the healing of leprosy.

Now we can better understand the magnitude of Jesus's specific miraculous healings of leprosy. I have loved the leper in this snapshot in Luke's Gospel since I was in college and discovered him for the first time. His leprosy would have required him to live alone, isolated and separate from community, and to call out, "Unclean! Unclean!" wherever he went in public (Lev. 13:45-46).

Can you imagine his shame? Can you feel his loneliness? Can you feel the desperation? Can you imagine living in a world where everyone moved away from you, kept his or her distance from you?

Understanding the first-century idea that only Messiah would be able to heal leprosy, we see that the leper's words to Jesus are stunningly vulnerable, raw, and full of messianic hopefulness. This man had leprosy, but he saw Jesus rightly and recognized Him as the long-awaited Messiah.

When he saw Jesus, he fell with his face to the ground and begged him,

> "Lord, if you are willing, you can make me clean."
> **LUKE 5:12b**

The leper didn't ask Jesus if He was *able* to heal him of leprosy. He asked Him if He was *willing*. The leper knew Jesus was able to do it because He was the Messiah. But what He didn't know just yet was Jesus's heart as God's Messiah. Power without compassion was the way of empire and the caesars. Power with compassion is the way of the kingdom of God.

How did Jesus respond to the leper's request? How does His response demonstrate both power and compassion?

Jesus met the leper in this moment with both power and compassion—the way of the kingdom of God. Jesus gave this leper the divine gift of His words and touch. Jesus moved toward him, reached for him, spoke to him, healed him, and sent him to the priests to fulfill levitical law.

Can you imagine being present for this moment? Jesus, the Galilean Rabbi, performed one of the four "biggies" in front of their eyes. Messiah had come. The kingdom of God was coming upon them in word and deed—in power that healed instead of ruled over them.

Stay tuned as we will see the other three messianic miracles later in our feast together.

FOUR MESSIANIC MIRACLES			
1	2	3	4
Healing of leprosy. Luke 5:13-14			

SNAPSHOT 3

Wreckage and Ruin, Restoration and Renewal

Two thousand years ago, there weren't too many things culturally worse than being a tax collector in Jesus's Jewish world. Tax collectors were considered somewhat perpetually unclean due to their close affiliation with Gentiles and for handling pagan money with pagan images on it on a regular basis. Tax collectors were not allowed to give testimony in court.[10] The life of a tax collector was a life of wreckage and ruin. The public and personal shame attached to being a tax collector was great—they were considered on the same level as prostitutes. The Talmud classified them alongside murderers and robbers.[11]

Rome exacted heavy taxes from the people groups she ruled over, Jews included. They often used local "middlemen" to do the dirty work of actually collecting the taxes for them. Tax collectors had a reputation for overcharging the people and pocketing the extra. They were also known for lending money with high interest rates to those who were not able to pay them back. Jews were not even allowed to take charity from a tax collector, and it was not considered a sin among the Jews to cheat a tax collector.[12]

What is the thing in your story that causes you to feel the most shame? What's that chapter in your life that you don't read out loud? You can answer this one in your head if writing it here is too much.

Imagine Jesus walking up to you in that moment. What do you think He would say to you?

The snapshot we are about to read answers this very important question. Jesus is the One who enters our wreckage and ruin to invite us into restoration and renewal.

READ LUKE 5:27-31.

This story is one of my favorites in all four Gospels. I read it often. It serves as a powerful picture of who Jesus is and what He is like. Levi, also known as Matthew, was "sitting at his tax booth" (v. 27). This language is so intimate—his tax booth, not just a tax booth. It's like Matthew and his tax booth were one. Matthew was deeply anchored in public, communal, and personal shame as a tax collector, and this story begins with Matthew actively doing that shameful thing.

Jesus isn't afraid of your wreckage and ruin.

Jesus walked up to Matthew at his worst, right in the middle of his deepest shame. Jesus met Matthew with an invitation to go somewhere and do something with Him. "Follow me," Jesus said to him (v. 27). Rather than judgment and condemnation, Jesus approached him with an invitation—to come out of his shame, and to enter into restored honor and acceptance in community. We learn something about Jesus here: Jesus meets us right where we are—but He never leaves us there.

Matthew's response to Jesus's invitation just makes me get teary. I can feel Him in this moment, in this story. The next line says, "and Levi got up, left everything and followed him" (v. 28). Matthew left his shame and accepted the invitation to enter into restoration and renewal. No longer a tax collector, now a disciple of Jesus.

It was incredibly unusual for rabbis to choose their disciples in the first-century Jewish world. But more than this, Jesus chose a tax collector to be one of His *talmidim*. If the story ended here, it would already be beautiful. But we're not finished yet, and the story gets even better. The invitation to restoration and renewal started spreading, and as we will see, it spread through table fellowship.

When we experience restoration, we become the agency of restoration for others.

Matthew left his tax collector's booth and hosted a great banquet for Jesus at his house. Rabbis did not eat with tax collectors in that world. Clean and unclean did not dine together. Jesus was inviting—welcoming, embracing, and accepting—not just Matthew the tax collector but "a large crowd of tax collectors and others" into his presence (v. 29). Jesus would eat with you.

The Pharisees asked Jesus's disciples about this highly unusual and suspect table fellowship affiliation—"Why do you eat and drink with tax collectors and sinners?" (v. 30).

Jesus Himself answered. What did He say? (See Luke 5:31-32)

How would you write Jesus's response in your own words?

With Jesus, the table of welcome is open to everyone, everywhere. There's a seat at His table for us; we just have to receive it.

This Matthew became one of the twelve disciples of Jesus. Years and years later, when Matthew was writing his Gospel, he used some specific words found in Matthew 10 that move me deeply. Matthew named the twelve disciples who were chosen by Jesus and received His invitation. He lists them: Simon, Andrew, James, John, Philip, and so forth. Then, he comes to writing his own name. But notice what he adds: "and Matthew the tax collector" (v. 3).

Of all the things he could have written about himself, he mentions he was a tax collector. His shame had been replaced by restoration, renewal, and honor. He could write about it because Jesus met him right in the middle of the shameful thing, the wreckage and ruin, and invited him into restoration and renewal.

You and I can find great hope in this story. Jesus chose a tax collector, so He will choose you and me. The table of welcome is open to us. We have a seat at Jesus's table.

SNAPSHOT 4

Sabbath

If you had a time machine and could travel back to be present in any biblical story with Jesus, which story/snapshot would you choose?

I often think about this question, and the answer sometimes changes based on what I'm currently studying or reading. More than anything though, if I had the chance to go back in time and spend a day with Jesus, I would choose any Sabbath.

Sabbath is other than, more than, and better than we think.

When you think of the word *Sabbath*, what's the first word that comes to your mind?

Our English word *Sabbath* comes from the Hebrew word *Shabbat* which means "to cease."[13] The heart of *Shabbat* is the command to cease our work so that we might remember God's work. What is that work? The living God is working a profound restoration—He's making everything new (Rev. 21:5). You and I woke up this morning into a world where the living God who does not slumber nor sleep has been making things new all night. While we slept, He was working. We woke up into active, divine, and holy restoration this morning.

Sabbath is a celebration of restoration. It is not passive. It is active. This is the reason I would choose to spend any Sabbath with Jesus. Jesus celebrated restoration on Sabbaths by healing people—bringing restoration to brokenness in the world. As you're reading through the Gospels, if it's a Sabbath and Jesus is present, you already know the story. Jesus is about to heal someone! He celebrated restoration by bringing restoration.

Let's take a look at one of these beautiful *Shabbat* stories of Jesus on a Sabbath in His first-century Jewish world.

READ LUKE 6:6-11 (THIS STORY IS ALSO FOUND IN MARK 3:1-6).

In Jesus's day, there was intense rabbinic debate about Sabbath and what constituted work that violated Sabbath. *Melakhah* was a Hebrew word used in Torah to specifically address activities prohibited on Sabbath.[14] In this passage we see that the Pharisees and teachers of the law were watching Jesus closely on the Sabbath day as the community gathered for their special Sabbath service.

The issue in this moment wasn't healing; it was whether Jesus would "work" in such a way that the Torah was violated in the way He healed (v. 7). Talk about missing the forest for the trees! The poor man with a shriveled hand woke up that morning and walked into that synagogue on Sabbath with no idea that Jesus would celebrate the restoration by restoring his right hand.

Jesus read the room and asked a direct, rabbinic question to the Pharisees: "I ask you, which is lawful on the Sabbath: to do good or to do evil, to save life or to destroy it?" (v. 9). The rabbis allowed for violation of Sabbath law when it came to matters of life and death. The Mishnah states, "Whenever there is doubt whether life is in danger, this overrides the Sabbath."[15] Jesus took this well-known principle of saving life and applied it to healing on the Sabbath.[16]

More about:

SABBATH

Sabbath is commanded twice in Torah: Exodus 20 and Deuteronomy 5. For the Jewish people, *Shabbat* is from sundown Friday night to sundown Saturday night. Two candles are lit at sundown on Friday night in remembrance of these two Sabbath commandments in Torah.[17]

Jesus went on to "completely restore" the man's right hand IN synagogue service ON the Sabbath. He brought a public, beautiful, and yet very personal restoration. I can feel the celebration in this moment—brokenness giving way to health and restoration. The kingdom of God was coming upon them in power, anchored in celebration. I'm telling you, if you somehow discover a time machine, go back and spend a Sabbath with Jesus!

Do you have Sabbath practices and rhythms in your life?

What would it look like for you to actively celebrate restoration?

From time to time, I invite people over on Friday night for dinner. We sit around the table—welcoming, embracing, and accepting each other. We tell our own, modern, right-now stories of how we are watching the living God bring restoration and make things new in our lives. Those dinners are so alive, joyful, and hopeful—full of flourishing and expectancy. They are some of my favorite nights of the year. Set your table. Invite your people to it. Light your lights, eat great food, and tell your restoration stories.

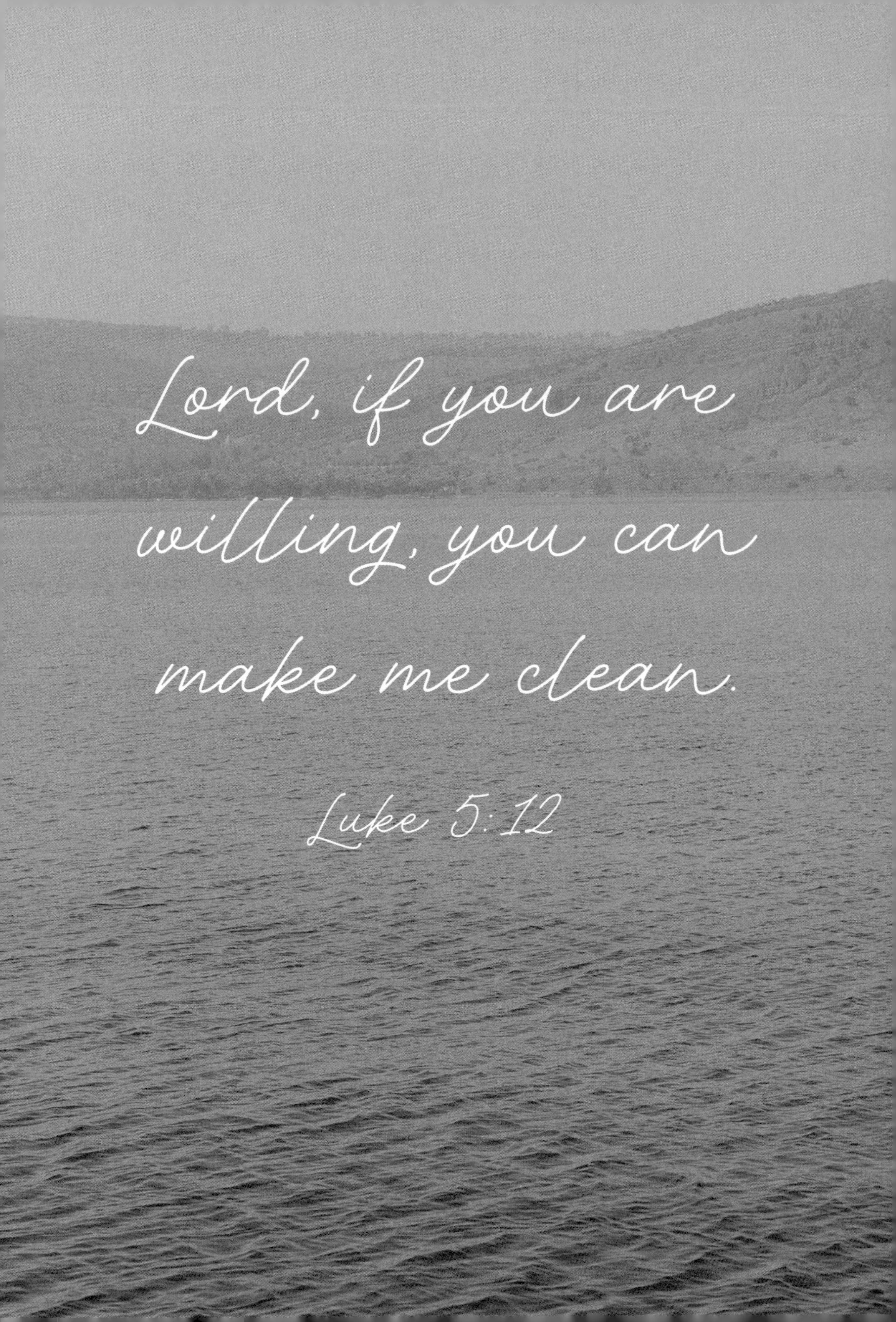
Lord, if you are willing, you can make me clean.
Luke 5:12

WATCH AND DISCUSS

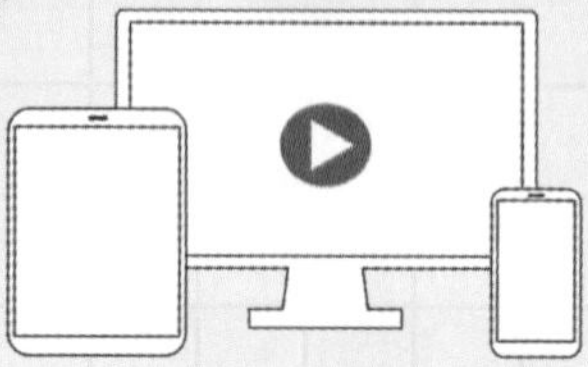

WATCH THE SESSION FOUR VIDEO. **Use the space below to take notes. Discuss the questions on the following page with your Bible study group. A more extensive leader guide is available for free download at lifeway.com/lukeintheland.**

To access the video sessions, use the instructions in the back of your Bible study book.

1. Read Luke 5:1-11 together. What did you learn about the disciples this session? How does that encourage you?

2. How did Jesus's response to the leper in Luke 5:13-14 demonstrate His character?

3. Share with the group how you wrote Jesus's response to the Pharisees in Luke 5:31-32 in your own words. What does that tell you about Jesus's mission?

4. What would it look like for you to celebrate restoration—as a group and as individuals—this week?

Session Five

PARTNERSHIP

With God, Not for God

Our snapshots for Session Five will focus on partnership. In Session Four we saw Jesus inviting men and women to follow Him. Now, we will see what that meant for those who said yes to His invitation. We sit with these snapshots because they show us what it's going to look like for those of us who have said yes to following Jesus in our own modern world.

To say yes to Jesus is to agree to take kingdom adventures as they find you. It's an agreement to partner with Him in bringing the kingdom of God to earth. This is seen in the Lord's Prayer, a prayer Jesus taught His disciples to pray and embody.

> . . . your kingdom come,
> your will be done,
> on earth as it is in heaven.
> **MATTHEW 6:10**

I have loved *The Chronicles of Narnia* since I was in college. The story captured my imagination and heart, and it has stayed with me ever since. I read the series every December; it's my annual Advent read. Remember my beloved quote?

> **WE MUST GO ON AND TAKE THE ADVENTURE THAT SHALL FALL TO US.**[1]
>
> C. S. LEWIS, *THE LAST BATTLE*

Years ago, a good friend of mine gave me a leather notebook cover engraved with this quote and my initials. I carry this notebook with me to all of my meetings and appointments, to Israel, and on all my trips. It is a constant reminder of my invitation to partner with Jesus, to agree with the Lord's Prayer, and to live as an agent of the kingdom of God in this world. I want Jesus to know He can count on me to take the adventures that fall to me!

One of the most encouraging, challenging, and hopeful things we see throughout all four Gospels is the way Jesus invited men and women to follow Him and partner with Him in proclaiming the kingdom of God and bringing heaven to earth. The disciples didn't simply watch or observe Jesus. We see snapshot after snapshot of them actively sharing in the ministry of moving kingdom into empire alongside Jesus.

Another way to see this is to say that the disciples learned to do things *with* Jesus, not *for* Jesus. Doing things for Jesus can feel lonely, burdensome, and even performative. Doing things with Jesus feels communal, energizing, and like shared togetherness toward a common goal.

Jesus modeled the way of the kingdom for His disciples.

Jesus lived the way of the kingdom with His disciples.

Jesus sent His disciples out to live the way of the kingdom and report back to Him.

Luke covers Jesus's final journey to Jerusalem uniquely and somewhat extensively in his Gospel record. This section of Scripture (Luke 9:51–19:44) is sometimes referred to as the "travel narrative" and it contains most of the content unique to Luke's Gospel.[2] It is a treasure chest of snapshots—stories, parables, teachings, healings, and exorcisms. The kingdom of God was coming close, and the kingdom of darkness was on the run.

READ LUKE 9:51. What word does your translation use to describe Jesus's journey to Jerusalem?

Jesus moved with purpose and intent, knowing He was headed to Jerusalem one final time before His crucifixion, resurrection, and ascension. As we journey through the travel narrative, we can see Jesus giving His last words, instructions, and teachings and partnering with His disciples to proclaim and bring the kingdom of God to earth through word and deed.

READ LUKE 10:1-3.

The partnership between Jesus and His disciples is seen in this snapshot. Jesus had already sent twelve disciples out (Luke 9:1-9). Here, He sent out seventy-two in pairs, or two-by-two, to "every town and place where he was about to go" (10:1).

They were the forerunners of His visitation to towns and villages from the Galilee, through Samaria and down into Judea, and ultimately to Jerusalem.

Why seventy-two? That number seems a bit specific. Some ancient manuscripts list seventy, not seventy-two. Jesus might have been referencing the story of Moses appointing seventy elders in Numbers 11:16,25-30. He also may have been referencing the Table of Nations in Genesis 10, as a way of indicating the spread of the gospel to all people.[3]

READ LUKE 10:4. Why do you think Jesus instructed His disciples in this way?

The details in this verse are incredibly interesting. The instruction not to take a purse, bag, or sandals sticks out to me. There is a simplicity and a difficulty in this adventure. Jesus was sending them out simply—they would travel light and need to rely on the hospitality of others along the way. Jesus was sending them out in difficulty as well—they were positioned in vulnerability as they entered towns and villages ahead of Jesus. They entered places humbly, dependent on the kindness of others rather than entering in pride and power.

There is yet another possibility here in the way Jesus sent out the seventy/seventy-two. The Mishnah gave instructions for people walking around in the temple courts in Jerusalem. Interestingly, one line says, "He may not enter into the Temple Mount with his staff or his sandal or his wallet . . ."[4] Jesus both instructed and modeled for His disciples and us today the way of His kingdom—a way that looks outward, moves outward, and invites all people to join God's family.

In Jesus's day, the temple in Jerusalem was the epicenter of Jewish life and worship. The people were a people of pilgrimage, "the ends of the earth" coming to Jerusalem to visit God's house and worship Him there. Could Jesus have been showing His disciples that the kingdom moved outward, even to the ends of the earth (Acts 1:8)? Was He showing them that everywhere they stepped foot was holy ground? That the kingdom was present and moving in power to save, redeem, and restore?

You and I are being sent out in simplicity and difficulty as well. We are a dependent, humble people. We rely on the Word of God to instruct us, and the Spirit of God to empower us to partner with the living God to bring heaven to earth. Word and Spirit have never failed a person, and you will not be the first. Let's go take the adventures that shall fall to us!

What are some of the kingdom of God adventures that have found you?

Are you on a kingdom adventure right now?

How have you seen others in your faith community partnering with the living God to bring heaven to earth?

Is there a way for you to support them? Encourage them? Partner with them in it?

The Finger of God

SNAPSHOT 2

As we make our way through the travel narrative, we come to another important snapshot in understanding the life and ministry of Jesus. This biblical snapshot is one of the four messianic miracles that were raised in the thoughts and awareness of the people in the first century. Remember from Session Four that we have already seen Jesus perform one of these four messianic miracles, in the healing of a person with leprosy. Today, we will see Jesus demonstrate His messianic power and authority by casting out a demon that was mute.

READ MATTHEW 12:22-28; MARK 9:17-29; AND LUKE 11:14-20.

Whose power did the people say Jesus was using to cast out the demon?

In Jesus's day, some rabbis and religious leaders could cast demons out of people. We see an example of this in Matthew 12:27. Jesus asked the Pharisees to tell Him by what power and authority they drove out demons. Clearly, some of them could do it.

History tells us they used a formula of asking the demon to give its name, and then they used the demon's name to drive it out.[5] We see Jesus using this first-century formula in Mark 5:9 when He was interacting with a man overtaken with demonic possession. He asked the demon to give its name. The demon answered, "My name

More about
THE MIRACLE

"A Roman legion had around five-thousand soldiers.

Rome's Tenth Legion's symbol was the boar.

Pigs were associated with pagan, cultic worship. The two-thousand pigs probably did not belong to personal or private family but more likely to a cultic site to worship the Roman emperor. Pigs can swim, so the drowning of the pigs in water was intentional and symbolic since the Decapolis was Gentile, Greco-Roman."[6]

is Legion" (v. 9). Then Jesus drove the demons out of the man and into pigs feeding nearby.

Now we are beginning to understand the difficulty in casting out a demon of muteness. This demon rendered a person possessed unable to speak; they were literally muted. When a rabbi or religious leader asked for the demon's name, the muted person was not able to answer, and therefore, they were unable to drive out the demon. This is exactly the kind of demon that the disciples could not drive out in Mark 9:17-18.

Now we are ready for our snapshot. The opening line is stunningly gorgeous to me. In a world where no one could cast out a mute demon, Jesus the Messiah showed up on the scene.

> Jesus was driving out a demon that was mute.
> **LUKE 11:14a**

> Here we go! Jesus cast out the demon of muteness and everyone was amazed. The Pharisees, however, attributed Jesus's power to the demonic. Jesus reasoned with them that Satan couldn't drive out Satan. He explained that the demonic couldn't drive out the demonic. That would be like a kingdom divided against itself.

Then Jesus explained that His power and authority to drive out the mute demon was by the finger of God. And because it was the finger of God, the "kingdom of God [had] come upon [them]" (v. 20).

The finger of God was a powerful image found in the Old Testament. The Egyptian magicians believed that the plagues on Egypt were miracles done by "the finger of God" (Ex. 8:19). Later, after God had delivered the Israelites out of

Egypt, He met them at Mount Sinai and gave them the two tablets of the covenant, which were inscribed "by the finger of God" (Ex. 31:18).

If the finger of God could touch one part of your life right now, what would you want it to be?

Just as the powerful finger of God had delivered the Israelites out of Egypt and given the covenant to God's people, Jesus was now equating His power to be able to cast out mute demons as the kingdom of God breaking forth in the earth. The same power that delivered the Israelites out of Egypt was present among the people in the person of Jesus. The Messiah and the Messianic age had finally arrived! And Jesus wasn't done yet. Remember, this is only the second of four messianic miracles. We will see the next two in the next two sessions.

I think about Jesus's heart in the way He walked this earth two thousand years ago—intentionally revealing through the four messianic miracles that He was indeed the long-hoped-for Messiah. I imagine that in these things, He wanted to be seen, chosen, and rightly accepted as the Savior of the world. A. W. Tozer once wrote, "He waits to be wanted."[7] I wonder what Jesus felt like as He was performing these particular miracles. I wonder if He felt a longing to be wanted. Sometimes when I open my Bible, I simply pray and say, "Lord, I want you. This is why I'm here."

Do you want Jesus? Tell Him. If your honest answer is no, tell Him that, too. Ask Him to help you to want Him more.

FOUR MESSIANIC MIRACLES			
1	2	3	4
Healing of leprosy. Luke 5:13-15	**Driving out a mute demon.** Luke 11:14-20		

✱ Surroundings of the Arbel National Park near the Sea of Galilee in Israel

SNAPSHOT 3

Partnership Through Generosity

As we continue to journey through the travel narrative, it is good to remember that Jesus was resolutely headed toward Jerusalem, toward His crucifixion and resurrection, and He knew it. The snapshots from Luke 9:51–19:44 show Jesus inaugurating the kingdom of God into a world of empire and partnering with His disciples to bring heaven to earth. After His ascension to heaven, His disciples would continue this work, empowered by the Spirit of God and informed by the Word of God.

Today we come to one of my all-time favorite verses in the entire Bible. I have loved it for years, and ponder and recite it often. For years, I kept this verse on a yellow sticky note on my bathroom mirror. I woke up to it. I went to bed to it. It is woven into the fabric of my heart and will be there forever. In my imagination, I can hear Jesus's tone of voice when He said it. In my imagination, I can feel what the disciples might have felt when He said it. For me, it's an important moment and an important snapshot in the gospel story.

> **Do not be afraid, little flock, for your Father has been pleased to give you the kingdom.**
> **LUKE 12:32**

Jot down how those words make you feel.

What emotions do you think the disciples felt upon hearing those words?

This verse has meant so much to me because, in many ways, I am a fearful person. Typically, my first response to kingdom adventures is fear—a knee-jerk reaction to back up, pull back, to abdicate. Thoughts flood my mind:

You can't do that.
You aren't ready for that.
Other people would do a much better job.
It's too risky.
You should just stay safe.
If you don't try, you can't fail.
Don't do it. It's beyond you.

The greatest battle for me as a disciple of Jesus is giving that initial yes in my heart to the kingdom adventure standing in front of me. This struggle is why this verse has come to mean so much to me.

Is it the same for you? What is your first response when a kingdom adventure finds you?

What are the thoughts that run through your mind?

The beautiful thing about this verse is it's embedded within a parable, an encouragement, and an embodied practice.

READ LUKE 12:13-21. This is the parable of the rich fool. What's the main teaching of this story?

READ LUKE 12:22-31. This is the encouragement. What is the directive to the disciples (and to us) from this snapshot?

READ LUKE 12:32. This is my verse! What do you learn about the character of God from just this one verse?

READ LUKE 12:33-34. This is the embodied practice. How would you rephrase this to apply to your world today?

The parable, the encouragement, and the embodied practice are all centered on the kingdom invitation to partner with Jesus in generosity. The empire mentality is anchored in scarcity and a fear that there won't be enough. Sometimes our stinginess or excessive storing up isn't rooted in greed. Sometimes it's rooted in fear. Jesus spoke to this in Luke 12:22-31. His kingdom is anchored in sufficiency and generosity.

As a professor who goes to Israel multiple times a year, one of my favorite lines in this section is, "Consider how the wild flowers grow" (v. 27). I was in Israel just a few months ago, and I took a photo of a flower growing out of hard rock on the Arbel Cliffs in the Galilee. I immediately thought of this verse and Luke 12:32.

Jesus is telling us to not be afraid because the Father is pleased to give us the kingdom! We can afford to spend our lives in partnership with Jesus to usher in the kingdom we receive from our Father. We are giving something being given to us. We can afford to live as open, generous people. We can actively live against the urge toward greed or striving and straining. And how do we live against it? By practicing generosity until we become generous people.

Responding to my fear with generosity is the only way I have been learning to "not be afraid." One day, I hope to wake up and find that generosity is a mature, spiritually formed muscle in my life and faith. I will just *be* generous like Jesus was generous. But until then, I'll keep practicing generosity because it's teaching me to not be afraid. My Father is pleased to give me the kingdom.

What helped you learn not to be afraid?

Who helped teach you not to be afraid?

Think of the most generous person you know and ask them what has cultivated that kingdom generosity in their lives.

I love the liturgy of generosity the Church of the City in New York recites together each week:

GENEROSITY LITURGY

"Holy Father, there is nothing I have that you have not given me. All I have and am belong to You, bought with the blood of Jesus. To spend everything on myself, and to give without sacrifice, is the way of the world that You cannot abide.

But generosity is the way of those who call Christ their Lord, who love Him with free hearts and serve Him with renewed minds. Who withstand the delusion of riches that chokes the word, whose hearts are in your kingdom and not in the systems of the world.

I am determined to increase in generosity until it can be said that there is no needy person among us. I am determined to be trustworthy with such a little thing as money that You may trust me with true riches.

Above all, I am determined to be generous because You, Father, are generous. It is the delight of Your daughters and sons to share Your traits, and to show what You are like to all the world.

Amen."[8]

* Surroundings of the Arbe National Park near the Sea of Galilee in Israel

SNAPSHOT 4

Celebration of Restoration

As we continue through the travel narrative, we are tracking along with Jesus and His disciples on their way to Jerusalem for one final time. As we talked about in Session Four, Jesus celebrated the Sabbath by bringing restoration.

Today we will see not one but two Sabbath healing snapshots with Jesus. They are located close together in the literary travel narrative. One is in Luke 13 and the other in Luke 14. Both snapshots immediately orient us to the fact that these things happened on the Sabbath.

READ LUKE 13:10-17. Whom did Jesus heal? How did the people react to this miracle?

READ LUKE 14:1-6. Whom did Jesus heal? Where was He when the miracle took place?

One healing happened in a synagogue. A woman who had been afflicted by a spirit for eighteen years and could not stand up straight was healed. The other healing happened in a Pharisee's home during a meal. A man was suffering from an abnormal swelling in his body, and Jesus healed him.

In both the synagogue and a private home, a woman and a man, Jesus celebrated the restoration of Sabbath by bringing healing and restoration. You can feel the goodness overflowing. The kingdom of God was coming upon them. I imagine Jesus waking up on Sabbath mornings smiling, grinning with restoration expectation.

One of the most amazing ways we can partner with Jesus in bringing heaven to earth is to cultivate meaningful Sabbath practices and rhythms. As we lay down our striving and straining and toil, we get a taste of the rest and restoration of heaven. We remember that we are more than what we produce or create. We remember that the most important work is God's work. We remember that He has been pleased to give us His kingdom. We cease. We remember. We celebrate.

Abraham Joshua Heschel wrote, "The Sabbath is a bride, and its celebration is like a wedding."[9] We have the opportunity to set our tables, invite others to them, and create *menuha* (rest) together.[10] We can rest, remember God's active restorative work, and celebrate it together. So many of us know how to work hard, hustle, and get things done. Are we skilled at meaningful, Sabbath rest? It too is a way we worship God. Heschel also wrote, "Labor is a craft, but perfect rest is an art."[11]

For the Jewish people, two *Shabbat* candles are lit at sundown on Friday night (the beginning of *Shabbat*). One candle is in honor of Exodus 20. The other is lit in honor of Deuteronomy 5. These are two places in the Torah where Sabbath was commanded.

READ EXODUS 20:8-11. **How did God lead by example in practicing the Sabbath?**

READ DEUTERONOMY 5:12-15. **Why does this passage say we should rest on the Sabbath?**

The honor of lighting the two *Shabbat* candles goes to the women. The woman of the house lights the candles and welcomes *Shabbat* into the home like a bride.

> When all work is brought to a standstill, the candles are lit. Just as creation began with the word, "Let there be light!" so does the celebration of creation begin with the kindling of lights. It is the woman who ushers in the joy and sets up the most exquisite symbol, light, to dominate the atmosphere of the home. And the world becomes a place of rest.[12]
>
> **ABRAHAM JOSHUA HESCHEL**

I hope we will grow in the art of Sabbath rest and become the agency of it for others. I pray we will grow and mature in celebrating the restoration. In this, we partner with the living God to bring heaven to earth.

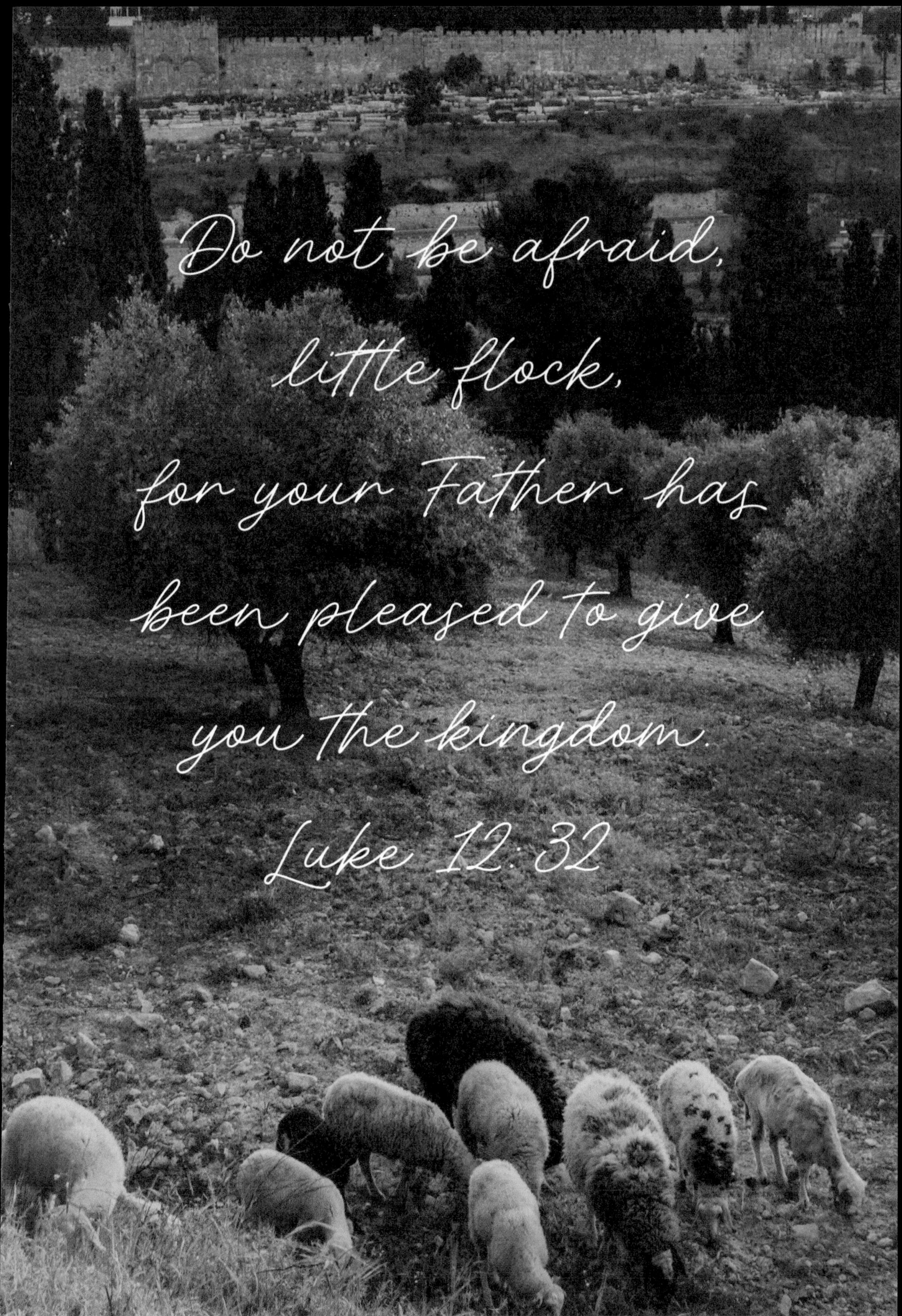
Do not be afraid,
little flock,
for your Father has
been pleased to give
you the kingdom.
Luke 12:32

WATCH AND DISCUSS

WATCH THE SESSION FIVE VIDEO. **Use the space below to take notes. Discuss the questions on the following page with your Bible study group. A more extensive leader guide is available for free download at lifeway.com/lukeintheland.**

To access the video sessions, use the instructions in the back of your Bible study book.

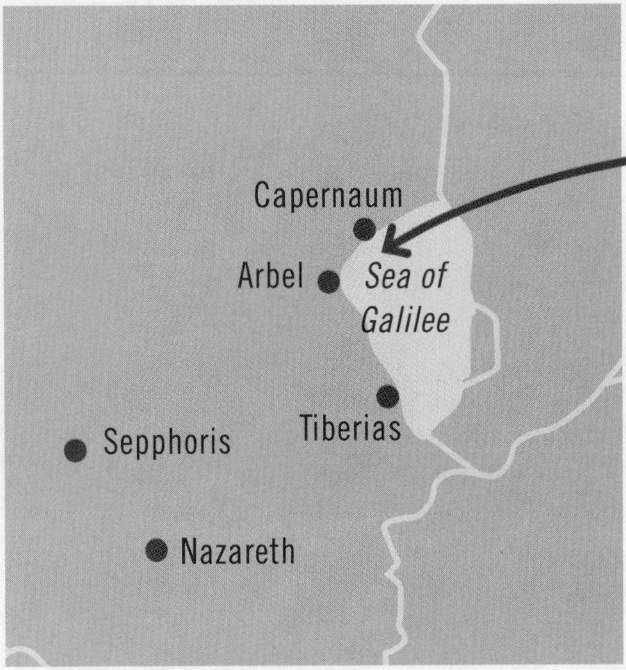

Arbel Cliffs

1. What kingdom adventures have you been a part of or witnessed in the lives of those around you?

2. Read Luke 11:14-20 and Matthew 12:22-28 as a group. With what power did Jesus cast out the demon?

3. Read Luke 12:32 together. What feelings do those words from Jesus provoke in you? How do you think the disciples felt hearing those words?

4. Who is the most generous person you know? How can you grow in generosity this week?

CRUCIFIXION

SNAPSHOT 1

A Man Born Blind

Our snapshots for Session Six will lead us to the crucifixion of Jesus. The travel narrative covered the intentional journey of Jesus not only toward Jerusalem but also toward the cross. We often think of the cross as something that happened to Jesus. Through these snapshots, we will see that Jesus happened to the cross. He demonstrated striking intentionality and faithful obedience as He went to the cross, hung on the cross, and eventually gave up His spirit to die for the sins of the world. Most of our snapshots this session will be found within the section of Luke's Gospel that follows the travel narrative, Luke 19:28–23:56.

Before we get there, it's time to unpack the third messianic miracle of Jesus. We have already covered two—the healing of leprosy, and the healing of a person possessed by a demon that rendered them mute. This third messianic miracle will help us better frame the days leading up to the crucifixion. We're going to take a small detour into the Gospel of John to find this snapshot.

In John 10:11, Jesus calls Himself the Good Shepherd, the One prepared to lay His very life down for His sheep. John 10 is a continuation of John 9; they go together as a unit, one snapshot. Jesus's identification as the Good Shepherd follows His third messianic miracle: the healing of a person born blind.

READ JOHN 9:1-12,32. What happened in this story?

No one had ever heard of this kind of miracle, so it was thought to be a miracle that only the Messiah could perform.[1] It happened in Jerusalem. And it happened on a Sabbath. As we've already learned, anytime we see a snapshot with Jesus and Sabbath we know what's going to happen. Jesus celebrated restoration by bringing restoration. Healing was on the way.

The third messianic miracle would surely have caused conversation all over Jerusalem, a hopeful stirring and wondering if the Messiah had truly arrived. Not only was this miracle performed in Jerusalem, but it also happened at one of the largest public pools in the city—the Pool of Siloam.

In first-century Jerusalem, there were two large public pools that probably served as places of ritual purification among other things. They were called the Pool of Bethesda and the Pool of Siloam. Crowds of people would have congregated at the pools. If you wanted all of Jerusalem talking about something, let it happen at one of those two pools. Word would have traveled fast throughout Jerusalem. We might think of those two pools serving as the news channels and social media of Jerusalem in the first century.

The Pool of Siloam was discovered in 2004. I've been told that it was an accidental find, that sanitation workers were working at the site and uncovered a section of the ancient pool. As I write this, further excavations are currently underway at the site in Jerusalem. When I take teams to Israel, we sit on the ancient steps of the Pool of Siloam, and we can feel its size and grandeur and imagine the crowds gathering there two thousand years ago.

The snapshot of John 9–10 begins with this one line—"As he went along, he saw a man blind from birth" (9:1). And off we go! Jesus made mud, put it on the man's eyes, and sent him to wash at the Pool of Siloam. It's so interesting to me that this miracle did not begin at the pool. Jesus sent the man to a very public, highly populated place to demonstrate His healing ability for a man born blind. It's almost as if Jesus wanted the public of Jerusalem to witness, to see, this miracle performed in their midst in Jerusalem.

READ JOHN 9:13-34. What was the reaction of the people and the Pharisees to the healing?

The man, blind from birth, came home seeing after washing in the Pool of Siloam, as Jesus had instructed him. This caused a ruckus among the people and the Pharisees. Nothing like this had ever happened in their history! The people debated the man's healing and took him to the religious leaders. The Pharisees questioned not only the man but his parents as well. They hotly debated this miracle performed in Jerusalem. Everyone wanted to understand what exactly had happened and what this meant.

This incredible healing story yielded one of the most beautiful lines in the whole Bible, given to us by the blind man whose sight was restored.

> He replied, "Whether he is a sinner or not, I don't know. One thing I do know. I was blind but now I see!"
> **JOHN 9:25**

READ JOHN 9:35-41.

This healing of a man born blind initiated a conversation between Jesus and the Pharisees about who could actually see. It's an upside-down story. The blind receive sight, while some of the religious leaders who should be able to see (meaning, rightly discern and understand) do not see. Jesus healed the man on the Sabbath, and the religious leaders regarded this as a violation of Sabbath laws. They could not understand how a Man who "broke the law" could carry such healing power. This conversation continues right into John 10.

READ JOHN 10:1-21. What or who does Jesus say He is in this passage?

Jesus presented Himself as the Good Shepherd—the One who would lay His life down for the sheep. But the spiritual shepherds of Israel, the Pharisees, could not celebrate the healing brought to a man born blind. They could not see what it meant, nor its value. Some of them missed the forest for the trees.

With three messianic miracles accomplished, Jesus would head to the cross, ready to lay down His life. The fourth messianic miracle would be on the other side of the crucifixion.

FOUR MESSIANIC MIRACLES			
1	2	3	4
Healing of leprosy. Luke 5:13-15	**Driving out a mute demon.** Luke 11:14-20	**Healing of a man born blind.** John 9:1-12,32	

SNAPSHOT 2

Finally, a Guest Room for Jesus

Today, our snapshot will be the Last Supper. This moment is written about in three of the Gospel letters.

READ AND COMPARE: MATTHEW 26:18, LUKE 22:14-15, AND JOHN 13:1.

This last meal with Jesus and His disciples was the calm before the chaos. From this Passover table, Jesus would intentionally move to the garden of Gethsemane, face arrest, rejection, trial, and crucifixion. The Last Supper was the last moment when everything was calm and quiet. And Jesus knew it.

Matthew, Luke, and John all mention that Jesus knew the crucifixion was coming. The words He shared with His disciples at the Last Supper were His last words before everything went down, so we can read them with the appropriate weight.

If you knew that your dinner with your family tonight was the last meal you would have with them, what would you say to them?

Your words would likely be meaningful and significant, the kind of words you would want to stay with them long after you were gone.

READ LUKE 22:7-20. What stands out to you from what Jesus says in this passage?

It was Passover in Jerusalem. It was time for the Passover lambs to be sacrificed. When I am in Jerusalem, I often think of all the lambs that would have been in Jerusalem two thousand years ago for this Passover festival. Meanwhile, Jesus, the Lamb of God, had come to die once-for-all as the ultimate and final sacrifice for sin.

Jesus sent Peter and John to make preparations for the Passover meal. They lived in Galilee but were in Jerusalem where they didn't have a home. Where would they meet for Passover? Jesus told them that they would see a man carrying a jar of water. This may sound strange, since so many people would have been flocking to Jerusalem for the Passover, and the streets would have been full of people. How would they possibly notice one man carrying a jar of water?

We might have a cultural clue here. Water fetching and carrying was typically a woman's work in that world. To see a man carrying a jar of water would have been unusual and likely would have stood out to Peter and John. Perhaps the man was an Essene, of the sect who most likely scribed the Dead Sea Scrolls at Qumran. As a predominantly male-only Jewish community, the men would have fetched and carried water for their community.

Regardless, they found the man and followed him to his home where they prepared for this final Passover meal together in his "guest room" (Luke 22:11). Bells and whistles should be going off for us here, as Luke is tying something together.

Where else have we seen Luke talk about a guest room?

This guest room in the house is the *katalyma* in Greek. It's the same word Luke used in Luke 2 for the birth story of Jesus in Bethlehem.[2] There was no room for Joseph and Mary in the *katalyma* or guest room of the home in Bethlehem.

Jesus did not have a *katalyma* (guest room) at His birth, but He would have one now for His final Passover meal with His disciples. Finally, Jesus got His guest room. Table fellowship in this *katalyma* would strengthen them all as they remembered, retold, and reimagined the Exodus story—the heart of Passover. Food and fellowship would shore them up for horrific events on the near horizon.

Have you ever had a memorable meal or conversation with a loved one? Perhaps it was the last conversation you had with them, or maybe it was simply an important moment in your relationship. What emotions and thoughts come to your mind as you remember their words? If it was a meal, what did you eat? Describe the moment here.

I often wonder about the disciples as they lived on past the crucifixion, resurrection, and ascension of Jesus. As they traveled the world, visiting places well outside of Judea, Samaria, and Galilee, did they remember this Last Supper often? Did they tell stories about the warmth, the comfort, and the celebration of that meal before the most important moments of human history occurred? Did they share the words Jesus shared with them? I like to think they carried this evening with them, and that His words and that meal provided light and warmth to their hearts in difficult times.

✷ Church of the Holy Sepulchre

Crucifixion in the Roman World

SNAPSHOT 3

Today our snapshot will be Luke's portrayal of the crucifixion of Jesus. It is one of the central signs of the upside-down kingdom of God moving in a world of power and empire. The central image, icon, and symbol of the Christian faith was the Roman Empire's symbol for its most shameful form of penalty and death.

The way of the kingdom and of Jesus is relinquishment. The way of empire is acquisition. The caesars sought to conquer, to acquire the world and set it under their domination and control. Jesus relinquished His very life to set the world free. He came to save and redeem the world from the bottom up—dying for the world so that, through faith in Him, the world would be renewed, restored, and freed. To follow Jesus is to lay your life down, trusting the living God to raise it up again.

Because of this, followers of Jesus understand that we often go down before we go up. Crucifixion precedes resurrection. Lament and celebration sit side by side. Grief and hope hold hands. As we head into the crucifixion, I hear John the Baptist's words ringing in my heart:

> Look, the Lamb of God, who takes away the sin of the world!
> **JOHN 1:29**

In a general sense, the practice of crucifixion began with the ancient Assyrians. It started as a primitive form of impalement since the Assyrians were not only conquerors but also torturers. The Romans later perfected crucifixion as the empire's vilest and most extreme form of penalty, punishment, and death.

Roman citizens and people of the upper class were, for the most, part exempt from crucifixion. It was reserved for foreigners, people of the lower classes, convicts, rebels, and slaves. Cicero, the ancient Roman lawyer, writer, and orator, called crucifixion the "cruel and disgusting penalty" and also the "extreme penalty."[3] This gives us insight into the different martyrdom deaths of two people in the Bible—Paul and Peter. Paul, a Roman citizen, was beheaded. Peter, a lower-class non-Roman citizen, was crucified.

Romans often crucified people along main roads for maximum exposure and impact. In a sentence, crucifixion spoke this to everyone passing by: *Defy Rome, and we will do this to you.* Crucifixion was a penalty and a deterrent to any longing for uprising, rebellion, or overthrow. Roman crucifixion usually followed three steps: scourging, carrying of the horizontal beam (*patibulum*) of the cross to the place along the road where the vertical beam (*stauros*) was already planted in the ground, and lifting. Some were tied to the cross. Others were nailed. Criminals were crucified in a row alongside the road.[4]

The crucified typically hung low to the ground. More well-known or high-status criminals were raised three feet above the ground. As people passed by, they would have been at almost eye-level, close up. Roman soldiers stood guard by the condemned day and night as travelers passed by bearing witness to the cruelty of Rome. They were guarding the criminals to keep them on the cross, keeping loved ones from approaching, comforting, or bringing aid to their loved ones. You could bear witness to your loved one hanging on a cross, but you couldn't physically get to them.[5]

Death by crucifixion could be swift, or it could take days. There are historical records of men talking from crosses, making legal contracts while hanging on a cross, and even being cut down after offering an acceptable bribe to one of the soldiers on guard. Some were hung in uniquely strange ways, including being crucified upside down.[6]

READ LUKE 23:26-43. Now that we've learned more about crucifixion in the Roman world, jot down your observations as you read through this passage. What do you notice?

Here are a few observations about Jesus's crucifixion within our historical understanding of Roman crucifixion.

1. Jesus most likely carried the *patibulum* (horizontal cross beam) before soldiers recruited Simon from Cyrene to carry it for him.

2. Jesus was most likely crucified at the base of Golgotha, not on it. There was a main road leading into and out of Jerusalem, and Jesus was probably crucified along that main road. People would have walked by, at eye-level as they hurled insults at Him.[7,8]

3. We see Jesus crucified with at least two other criminals on each side. We might well imagine more.

4. Roman soldiers were present, guarding Jesus as He was crucified. His mother, Mary was present. She could watch, but she could not touch Him. She could bear witness to His agony, but she could not get to Him to cover, comfort, or feed Him. Can you even begin to imagine this?

5. Roman soldiers cast lots for His clothing. This imagery is found in Psalm 22:18. This also might indicate that Jesus would have been crucified naked—another humiliation of crucifixion was often exposure. Christian art covers Jesus when portraying Him on the cross. This was probably not a kindness given by the Romans in reality.

End your time with this snapshot in prayer. Thank God for sending His Son to relinquish His life for yours. Thank Jesus, the Good Shepherd, for His sacrifice. And praise God that this is not the end of the story!

SNAPSHOT 4

Grief and Hope Hold Hands

Today we will continue our snapshot of the crucifixion of Jesus within the Jewish cultural context of two thousand years ago. We pick up the story from yesterday with Jesus, the Lamb of God, hanging on a Roman cross.

READ LUKE 23:44-49. **Write down your observations.**

Today we will see the intentionality of Jesus and the grief of God the Father. The details of the crucifixion start to carry deeper meaning when we look closer. Gospel authors gave great detail in communicating the timing of the crucifixion of Jesus. They made sure we knew what time Jesus went onto the cross, as well as what time He gave up His spirit. So, we know that Jesus spent approximately six hours on the cross. Why do these details matter?

MORNING AND EVENING SACRIFICES

Mark 15:21-25 tells us that Jesus went onto the cross at 9 a.m.—the time of the early morning sacrifice. Luke 23:44-46 tells us that Jesus breathed His last at 3 p.m.—the time of the evening sacrifice. The 9 a.m. and 3 p.m. times of sacrificing lambs were called the *tamid* sacrifices. *Tamid* means "continual" or "perpetual" or "ongoing."[9] These were two significant daily times within ancient Jewish religious life.

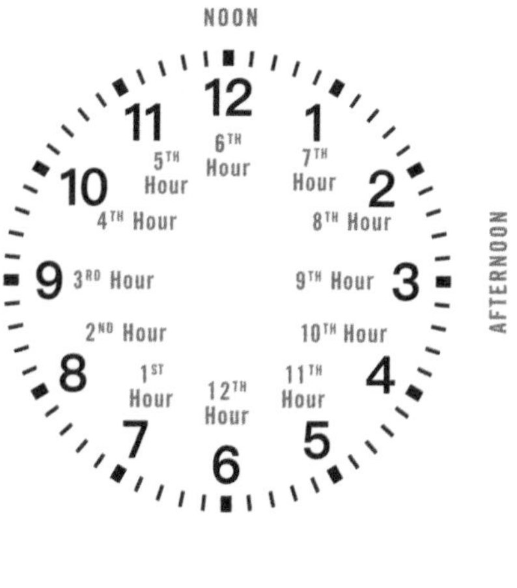

TURN TO EXODUS 19:38-42. How often were the sacrifices to be made?

Jesus was fulfilling the *tamid* sacrifices once and for all—the perfect Lamb of God, being sacrificed at 9 a.m. and 3 p.m. We do not know all of the reasons for Jesus being on the cross for six hours, but the significance of the *tamid* sacrifices gives us a strong indicator. He fulfilled the 9 a.m. morning sacrifice and hung on the cross long enough to also fulfill the 3 p.m. evening sacrifice. We often think of the cross happening to Jesus. Here, we get a glimpse of Jesus happening to the cross. It was the instrument through which Jesus would totally, completely, and forever fulfill the *tamid* sacrifices before a holy God.

At 3 p.m., Jesus gave up His spirit and breathed His last. Luke mentioned that at that very moment, the "curtain of the temple was torn in two" (Luke 23:45). This was no ordinary curtain. This was a curtain of enormous size and weight that hung in the temple in Jerusalem. Exodus 26 describes the curtain as being multi-colored with blue, scarlet, and purple. The Mishnah described it as follows.

> The veil was one handbreadth thick and was woven on [a loom having] seventy-two rods, and over each rod were twenty-four threads. Its length was forty cubits and its breadth twenty cubits; it was made by eighty-two young girls, and they used to make two in every year; and three hundred priests immersed it.[10]

Matthew gave us more details in his Gospel account of this 3 p.m. moment when Jesus gave up His spirit and the curtain split. He carefully wrote, "At that moment the curtain of the temple was torn in two from top to bottom" (27:51). At the very moment when Jesus breathed His last and died, the enormous curtain in the temple was torn "from top to bottom."

What do you think is the significance of the curtain tearing? What about the way it was torn?

Over my time in the Holy Land through the last seventeen years, I have heard stories of grief, lament, and heartache. Most cultures have rhythms and practices of lament, outward signs of hearts broken within. I have been told that sometimes women beat their breasts in grief and lament. And I have also been told that sometimes men tear their shirts from top to bottom in grief and lament. This might follow the ancient practice of rending garments as outward signs of pain, hurt, and lament.

If you were in Jesus's world two thousand years ago, you might recognize the rending of the curtain as a sign of grief, lament, or bearing witness to pain. Only God could have torn such a curtain. Especially from top to bottom.

It is a profound thought to me that God would show signs of grief and lament in this moment. We know from Scripture that God does grieve.

READ THE FOLLOWING PASSAGES OF SCRIPTURE.
What does God grieve over?

☐ **Genesis 6:5-6**

☐ **Psalm 78:40**

☐ **John 11:33-35**

☐ **Ephesians 4:25-30**

Grief is one of the many emotions God models for us, alongside emotions like love and joy. Knowing God Himself grieves, how does that change the way you think about your own grief?

READ 1 THESSALONIANS 4:13. **What does that tell you about grief for those who follow Jesus?**

Grief can be endured because it holds hope's hand. We too can afford to go down, to reckon our hurts, pain, and brokenness knowing that our deepest grief is mingled with our highest hope. We suffer but for a little while. The new heaven and new earth are on the way. We can courage up and courage into hard things, refusing to avert our eyes and look away. We go through grief and lament *with* hope, not until we find hope. Grief and hope are companions who accompany us on the journey of life. As we well know, Luke's Gospel doesn't end with the crucifixion of Jesus. Our stories won't end in grief and lament either.

Not only did the curtain perhaps remind people of grief, but it also signaled a much more significant moment for those watching these events take place. The great curtain in the temple hung as a dividing partition between the holy place and the most holy place (the holy of holies). In other words, behind the veil sat the ark of the covenant and the presence of God (Ex. 25:10-22). The curtain was like a robe, veiling Him in holiness and separateness. Only a select few—the high priests—were ever allowed to enter into the room of God's presence. When Jesus died, the veil was torn in a way that only God could have torn it. There was no longer a boundary between the presence of God and the people. Grief and hope holding hands. Jesus came for everybody, y'all. We are all invited into His presence.

WATCH AND DISCUSS

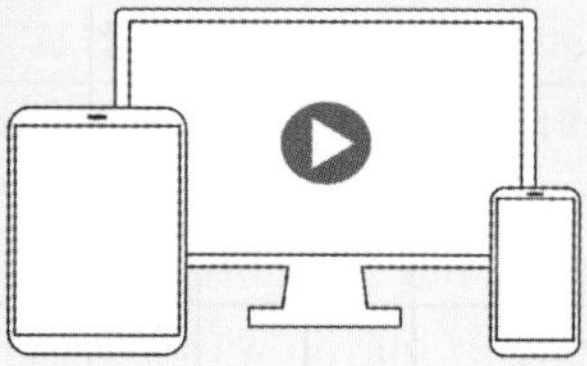

WATCH THE SESSION SIX VIDEO. Use the space below to take notes. Discuss the questions on the following page with your Bible study group. A more extensive leader guide is available for free download at lifeway.com/lukeintheland.

To access the video sessions, use the instructions in the back of your Bible study book.

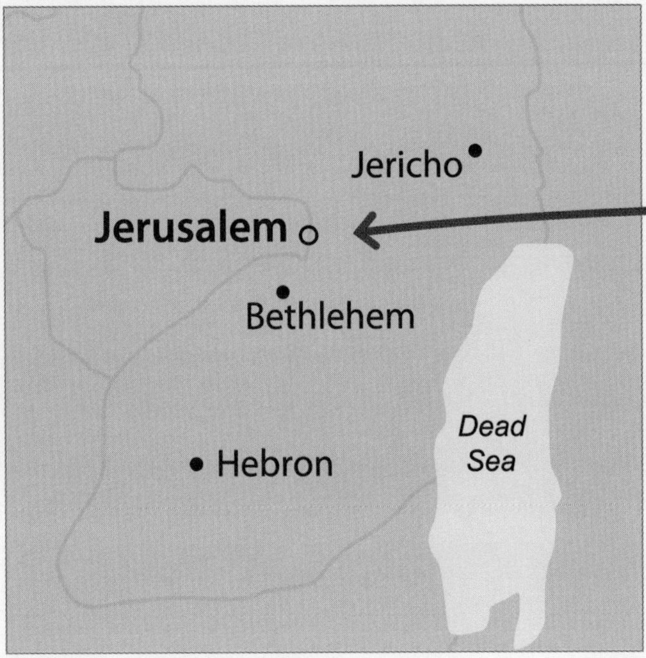

Garden of Gethsemane

Southern Steps

1. Read John 10:1-18. Which of these metaphors for who Jesus is encourages you the most today? Share why.

2. Describe the meal or the moment you wrote about in Snapshot 2. Why was that time significant for you?

3. What from Snapshot 3 regarding crucifixion stood out to you, after reading about crucifixion in the Roman world? How does it change or enhance the way you look at Jesus's sacrifice for you?

4. Grief is one of the many emotions God models for us, alongside emotions like love and joy. Knowing God Himself grieves, how does that change the way you think about your own grief?

RESURRECTION

SNAPSHOT 1

Women of Resurrection & Pilgrimage

Our snapshots for Session Seven will center on the resurrection of Jesus. The two most important events in human history, Jesus's death and resurrection, happened in and right outside of Jerusalem. Luke emphasized the presence of women in the crucifixion, burial, and resurrection of Jesus. They bore witness to the agony of the crucifixion. They prepared spices and perfumes for Jesus's body in the grave. And they were the first eyewitnesses and proclaimers of the resurrection. They were there—fully present and engaged.

As someone who has been taking teams to Israel since 2008, I always love each day that I get to spend in Jerusalem. She has seen so much throughout human history. She endured the Babylonian invasion in 586 BC when the city of Jerusalem was conquered and Solomon's temple was destroyed. She endured Roman invasion in AD 70 when the city was devastated and Herod's temple was destroyed. To date, the temple has never been rebuilt.

For all that Jerusalem has seen over thousands of years, she is also the home of the death, burial, and resurrection of Jesus. The Church of the Holy Sepulchre in Jerusalem is the most likely historical location for the burial and resurrection of Jesus. And we have a woman to thank for the building of this large church that marks and commemorates the burial and resurrection of Jesus.

Helena, the mother of the emperor Constantine, led a pilgrimage to Palestine in the AD 320s with unlimited imperial resources. She is credited with building and decorating several churches and monuments at holy sites, as well as being a generous giver of alms to the poor. When you visit the Holy Land and go to the Church of Nativity in Bethlehem, you are visiting a church originally built by Helena (it has been destroyed and rebuilt a few times). When you visit the Church of the Holy Sepulchre in Jerusalem, you are also visiting a church built by Helena (it has been modified throughout the years).[1]

It is beautiful to me that women were central in the historical events of the crucifixion, burial, and resurrection of Jesus and in pilgrimage journeys and adventures, contributing to the pilgrimage experience of millions of people who come to the Holy Land to visit the very sites of the biblical stories. We are the current living generations of the church. It's our turn to live fully present and engaged in the kingdom-of-God work of following Jesus and making him known.

How have women played a part in carrying forth the gospel in your life? Jot down a few names of those who have borne witness to you of the good news of Christ—maybe you can think of a Sunday School teacher, a Bible study friend, a neighbor, or a family member.

If you have contact information for the names listed above, consider sending them a quick text or note to let them know you're thankful for them.

Today, we pick up the storyline right where we left off last time in Luke's Gospel.

READ LUKE 23:50-56. **What specific details did you notice after the previous session's study?**

After Jesus's death on the cross, Joseph of Arimathea was the first to courage up and courage into participating in the story of Jesus's burial. He went to Pilate and "asked for Jesus' body" (v. 52). This affiliation with Jesus could have led to Joseph's arrest as a sympathizer of Jesus.

We don't often think about Joseph of Arimathea physically removing Jesus's body from the cross. Joseph would have moved past seeing into experiencing the gruesomeness of the cross as he lowered the scourged, beaten, bloodied, and crucified body of Jesus off of the cross. What did it feel like to loosen the nails out of the wood? What was it like to hold the body of the Messiah, the Lamb of God? Did he cry and wail, or was he quiet in stunned silence? What was he feeling?

Luke went on to tell us that Joseph took Jesus's body and "wrapped it in linen cloth and placed it in a tomb cut in the rock" (v. 53). This would have been a stone-rolled *kokhim* tomb in the first century. Families would build burial chambers with multiple individual niches, or *kokhes,* cut into the rock where they could lay their dead.[2] When visiting Israel, you can still see ancient stone-rolled *kokhim* tombs.

What are the funeral and burial customs in your culture, or the culture where you live?

How do those customs shape the way you think of Jesus's death and burial?

The women followed Joseph and saw the family tomb where he laid Jesus in one of the *kokhes,* or burial niches. Sabbath was on the way, so they went home to prepare the spices and perfumes to finish the burial rites for Jesus after the Sabbath in order to avoid violating the Sabbath.

Later on, we will pick up with these women going to visit the tomb to dress Jesus's body with spices and perfumes. They did not know that they would be the most unused and irrelevant burial spices and perfumes in all of human history.

SNAPSHOT 2

All Things Resurrection

Before we move to the resurrection of Jesus, it's time to discover the fourth messianic miracle of Jesus. We have covered three so far—the healing of leprosy, the healing of a person possessed by a demon that rendered them mute, and the healing of a person born blind. This fourth messianic miracle was a tremor of a greater miracle yet to come.

We're going to look at a snapshot that happened before Jesus was crucified—we're going to talk about the resurrection before His resurrection. John told us about this snapshot in his Gospel when we see Jesus raise Lazarus from the dead. This was the fourth messianic miracle performed by Jesus.[3]

READ JOHN 11:1-43. Note below all the characteristics or attributes of God you can see Jesus displaying in this story.

Lazarus lived in Bethany, just two miles from Jerusalem. Jesus intentionally arrived in Bethany four days after Lazarus had been laid in the tomb. The Pharisees believed that a person's spirit hovered or lingered near the body for three days, making resuscitation possible. Jesus raising Lazarus on the fourth day made it a certain miracle of resurrection. With Bethany being so close to Jerusalem, word would have traveled fast throughout the city.

It was unnerving to the religious leaders in Jerusalem that this kind of messianic power was on display just two miles away in Bethany. They responded with a bold plan—they started plotting to kill Jesus (John 11:45-57). In the end, this messianic miracle was a tremor of another resurrection, the resurrection of Jesus.

FOUR MESSIANIC MIRACLES			
1	2	3	4
Healing of leprosy Luke 5:13-15	**Driving out a mute demon** Luke 11:14-20	**Healing of a man born blind** John 9:1-12,32	**Raising Lazarus from the dead** John 11:1-43

READ LUKE 24:1-12. **Who went to the tomb first?**

Luke 24 begins with the women taking burial spices and perfume they would never use to the tomb of Jesus. Two angelic messengers met them in the empty tomb. I often wonder if we will get to meet these two angels in heaven and ask them what it was like to be sent to deliver the resurrection message to these women. It reminds me of Gabriel visiting young Mary and telling her she will give birth to the long-awaited and much hoped-for Messiah. With one question and two facts, they explained the empty tomb.

> Why do you look for the living among the dead? He is not here; he has risen!
> **LUKE 24:5-6**

The women returned to the eleven disciples and the others and shared the good news. I love Luke for naming them here, again emphasizing the feminine presence and feminine proclamation of the resurrection. They were the original harbingers of resurrection, and Luke took the time to name them. One was Mary Magdalene. The woman who had seven demons cast out of her, followed and supported Jesus's ministry, bore witness to the crucifixion, and prepared spices and perfume for His burial was also the first to experience the risen Jesus.

READ JOHN 20:1,11-18.

In John's Gospel, he centralized Mary as the one who went to the tomb, found it empty, and was the first to witness and also to interact with the risen Lord. John uses a literary device to show us a bigger picture in the interaction. Jesus, raised from the dead, spoke first to Mary. But she did not know it was Jesus. John tells us that she thought "he was the gardener" (v. 15).

Can you think of another time when a woman talked with God in a garden?

Eve. In the garden of Eden. She and Adam ate the fruit and their eyes were opened to nakedness and shame. Their sin brought death into the world.

Here Mary is, talking with the God of the universe in a garden housing tombs, and her eyes are opened to the resurrected Jesus. It's a redemptive moment in the overarching story of the Bible. We, too, have had our eyes opened to our shame and sin. And we too have had our eyes opened to the real hope of our resurrection made possible through Jesus's resurrection.

When I take teams to Israel, we visit an ancient coastal city on the western shore of the Sea of Galilee called Magdala, or Migdal. It was an important fishing village in the first century. Salted fish from Magdala were shipped throughout the Roman Empire. It's the traditional home of Mary Magdalene—Mary of Magdala or Mary of Migdal.

To date, archaeologists have discovered one ancient first-century synagogue at Migdal and potentially a second one. Every time I stand in front of that first-century synagogue, I imagine Jesus teaching there. He went around the Galilee, teaching in their synagogues, healing the sick, and casting out demons (Matt. 4:23-25). It is one of my absolute favorite sites to visit with teams.

✱ The Mosaic at Migdal shows Jesus and Mary Magdalene. Notice the seven demons coming off of her as Jesus is reaching for her and she's reaching for Him. This mosaic is located in a chapel at Migdal that is completely dedicated to women.

Because it is the traditional home of Mary of Migdal, a chapel was built on the site to honor the women of the Bible. When you walk into the central chamber, there are beautiful columns with the names of women in the Bible engraved on them. There is one column standing that is left blank. It represents you and me. It stands there in acknowledgment of feminine faith today and our devotion to Jesus.

At the entrance you will read these words,

> In this Holy place the Church gives thanks to the Most Holy Trinity for the mystery of woman, and for every woman, for her eternal dignity and for the wonders God has worked in and through her in the history of humanity.

As we learned in Session Two, *migdal* is a Hebrew word meaning "tower." Magdala is an Aramaic word meaning "tower."[4] We have known Peter as "the Rock." Mary was "the Tower." If I could have a cup of coffee with either Peter or Mary, I would choose Mary every single time. She saw things Peter didn't see. She experienced things Peter didn't experience. It moves me deeply that her same eyes that refused to look away at the crucifixion were given the honor of being the first eyes to see the resurrected Jesus.

SNAPSHOT 3

Revealing & Explaining

Today our snapshots will be the continuation of the resurrection of Jesus. Have you ever really paid attention to what Jesus chose to do after His death, burial, and resurrection? After conquering death and opening up the promise of eternal life for all who believe, what did Jesus choose to do with His remaining days on earth before His ascension back to His Father in heaven?

Luke 24, the last chapter of Luke's Gospel, reveals some of Jesus's final earthly activities. Yesterday we saw Mary Magdalene's eyes opened in the garden tombs and reflected that it was the second time a woman had talked to God in a garden and had her eyes opened (Eve). Today, more eyes will be opened. More will see the resurrected Jesus and interact with Him. Part of being participants in the coming kingdom of God on earth as it is in heaven is to agree to see. We are learning to look, pay attention to the movement of God in this world, and seek to engage the world.

Jesus spent His last days on earth doing two things: revealing and explaining. He intentionally sought out His disciples and revealed Himself to them, opening their eyes to see. He also explained the reality of the crucifixion and resurrection within the overarching story of the Bible—the Torah and the Prophets. He opened their eyes to Him and the Word of the Lord. The living Word was explaining the written Word in a way that helped them see that they were living out the fulfillment of the story of the Bible. They would be the witnesses to the world about the life, death, and resurrection of Jesus.

READ LUKE 24:13-32.

I love the opening line of this snapshot: "Now that same day . . ." The very day that Jesus rose from the dead, He not only opened the eyes of Mary, "the Tower," but He opened the eyes of two disciples on an ancient road heading to Emmaus from Jerusalem. Just as Mary did not initially recognize Jesus in the garden tomb, these two did not initially know that it was Jesus who walked with them along the road.

The two were resigned to what they had seen, the death of Jesus. And they walked with broken hearts; ". . . but we had hoped" was their disposition and mood (v. 21). The resurrected Jesus walked with them, but they could not yet see. In this snapshot, Jesus chose to explain and then to reveal. He started explaining the Torah and the Prophets, explaining to them what was said in all the Scriptures concerning Himself. Word made flesh was putting flesh to the written Word, integrating the prophetic promises with the fulfillment in His very resurrected presence among them.

As He entered their home and shared a meal that very resurrection night, He broke bread, and their eyes were opened. Unlike Eve and very much like Mary, their eyes were opened to the resurrected Jesus, sitting at their table, eating their food. When they recognized Him, He vanished. But not for long. There were more who needed to see and understand.

READ LUKE 24:33-53. How did the disciples react to Jesus's appearing?

In this snapshot, Jesus chose to reveal and then explain. The two in Emmaus who had just had their eyes opened went back to Jerusalem to tell everyone what had just happened. I imagine them running. I imagine them crying. How exactly would the human heart have even taken in such an incredible moment? For the rest of their lives, as they sat at that table and ate their meals, they would have remembered that time the resurrected Lord broke bread at that very table and the feeling of having their eyes opened.

Later, while these two were in the middle of telling a larger group what had just happened, Jesus just showed up in their midst with a simple greeting, "Peace be with you" (v. 36). The words Luke used to describe their reactions were "startled" and "frightened," and we might add confused, since they thought He was a ghost (v.37). They could not take in the magnitude of the resurrection. The joy and amazement of it was too much for them. You can almost feel the surging joy and kingdom celebration as the resurrected Jesus asked them for something to eat. Jesus practiced meaningful table fellowship His whole earthly life and ministry, including His resurrection appearances.

As Luke ends His Gospel, but not His writings (Acts is next), two lines begin to reveal and explain the rest of the New Testament writings and story to both those gathered then and to us now.

READ LUKE 24:45-48. Write out Luke 24:48 below.

What were the disciples witnesses of?

You and I are having our eyes opened more and more as we walk with Jesus and as the Spirit of God reveals the Scriptures to us. We are the current witnesses in the world to these things. Jesus is being revealed and explained to the world through us.

The disciples were eyewitnesses to the earthly life, death, burial, and resurrection of Jesus. How can we be eyewitnesses to Jesus's character and works today?

SNAPSHOT 4

Tikkun Olam

Today we come to our final snapshot for this series. We have seen many snapshots throughout Luke and other portions of the Bible, and they have been teaching us who Jesus is, what He is like, and what will it mean for us to accept His invitation to follow and partner with Him in bringing the kingdom into a world of empire. As discussed in Session One, Luke–Acts was originally a part one and part two, writings that were intended to be read together. Our final snapshot will honor this by moving into Acts 1 to string the pearl of Luke with the pearl of Acts. We will not end with Luke 24 because the story didn't end there. There was more to come after Jesus's earthly life, death, burial, and even His resurrection.

READ ACTS 1:1-3. Does anything stand out to you in these verses after having studied the "former book" of Luke?

Luke begins Acts with a summary of his previous gospel work in three simple yet powerful verses. Jesus's earthly ministry was one of word (teaching) and works (doing). He was the Word made flesh, dwelling among the people and inaugurating the kingdom of God. He was the fulfillment of Isaiah's prophecy in Isaiah 9 and started inviting men and women to partner with Him in bringing heaven to earth, the kingdom of God into a world of empire.

There is one line within this passage that has been ruling and reigning in my heart for the last several months. The day I started writing this series, I knew I was going to end it by writing about this one line in Acts 1. I keep thinking about it, pondering it on my early morning walks with Chester, talking about it with my friends and community, and imagining what it would have been like to witness it two thousand years ago.

How long did Jesus appear to the apostles after His resurrection?

Bells and whistles are going off for us now when we read that the resurrected Jesus appeared to His disciples for forty days. As we have already learned, forty represents fulfillment and change throughout the story of the Bible. Remember, when you see forty, look for change. And here, Luke carefully tells us that Jesus appeared to them for forty days. Change is on the way.

I have been spending time pondering those forty days lately. Of all the things Jesus could have talked about during those appearances and visitations after His resurrection, Luke tells us one thing that Jesus chose to talk about over and over again—the kingdom of God. Jesus, who had just defeated sin, death, hell, and grave, was thinking about the kingdom of God.

What do you think those conversations sounded like?

What do you imagine was the tone in His voice?

What was His demeanor as He sat, ate, and talked with the apostles?

What were their questions, and how did He answer them?

Why talk about the kingdom of God? Because what Jesus had done during His earthly ministry—words and works—His disciples would now do through the power of the Holy Spirit. They would continue this work of bringing heaven to earth, of bringing the kingdom of God into a world of empire. The story continued.

And the story is still going—it includes you and me, today, right now, in our everyday lives.

The Jewish people have a phrase that has captured my heart and attention over the last year. It's the *tikkun olam*—the "repair of the world" or the "fixing of the world."[5] For the Jews, the invitation is to engage the world, not retreat from it.

The Jewish people are living out the mandate given to their ancestors Abraham and Sarah in Genesis 18:19—to do what is just (*mishpat*) and right (*tzedakah*). They are engaging the world to heal it, to better it, to embody the work of *tikkun olam*.

How can you engage in and embody the work of *tikkun olam* in your everyday life?

Luke–Acts is inviting us to partner with Jesus in engaging the world in personal and collective ways, sanctifying our everyday lives with godly goodness as we are empowered by the Spirit and informed by the Word of God. As we follow Jesus and partner with Him in kingdom work, others will be inspired to know the One true God—the God of Abraham, Isaac, and Jacob; the God of Luke, Matthew the tax collector, and Mary "the Tower." We, too, seek to be kingdom agents of *mishpat* (justice) and *tzedakah* (righteousness) in this world—to see heaven come to earth and kingdom move into empire.

Let's "go on and take the adventure that shall fall to us!"[6]

WATCH AND DISCUSS

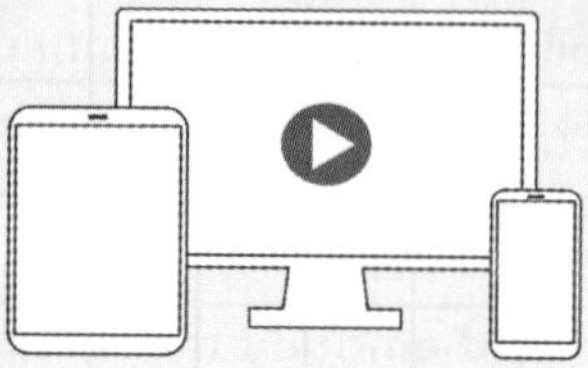

WATCH THE SESSION SEVEN VIDEO. **Use the space below to take notes. Discuss the questions on the following page with your Bible study group. A more extensive leader guide is available for free download at lifeway.com/lukeintheland.**

To access the video sessions, use the instructions in the back of your Bible study book.

Tiberias (home setting)

Road to Emmaus

1. How have women played a part in carrying forth the gospel in your life? Share some stories with the group.

2. Look back at John 11 as a group. What characteristics or attributes of God did you see Jesus displaying in this story?

3. The disciples were eyewitnesses to the earthly life, death, burial, and resurrection of Jesus. How can we be eyewitnesses to Jesus's character and works today?

4. How can you engage in and embody the work of *tikkun olam* in your everyday life?

Notes

Notes

Luke Reading Plan

The Gospel of Luke tells us the story of Jesus's time on earth through a series of snapshots, similar to how we collect photos in an album. Luke doesn't recount every moment of Jesus's life, but instead, he highlights some important moments for us. During our time together, we'll study some of those snapshots, but a comprehensive, verse-by-verse study of the book of Luke is not within the scope of this study. If you'd like to take the time to read the entire Gospel of Luke as you study, we've provided a supplementary reading plan for you. Happy reading!

SESSION ONE

- ☐ Luke 1:1-56
- ☐ Luke 1:57-80
- ☐ Luke 2
- ☐ Luke 3

SESSION TWO

- ☐ Luke 4
- ☐ Luke 5:1–6:19
- ☐ Luke 6:20-49
- ☐ Luke 7

SESSION THREE

- ☐ Luke 8:1-21
- ☐ Luke 8:22–9:17
- ☐ Luke 9:18-62
- ☐ Luke 10

SESSION FOUR

- ☐ Luke 11
- ☐ Luke 12:1-34
- ☐ Luke 12:35–59
- ☐ Luke 13

SESSION FIVE

- ☐ Luke 14
- ☐ Luke 15
- ☐ Luke 16
- ☐ Luke 17

SESSION SIX

- ☐ Luke 18:1-30
- ☐ Luke 18:31–19:10
- ☐ Luke 19:11-48
- ☐ Luke 20:1–21:4

SESSION SEVEN

- ☐ Luke 21:5-38
- ☐ Luke 22:1-62
- ☐ Luke 22:63–23:56
- ☐ Luke 24

Map

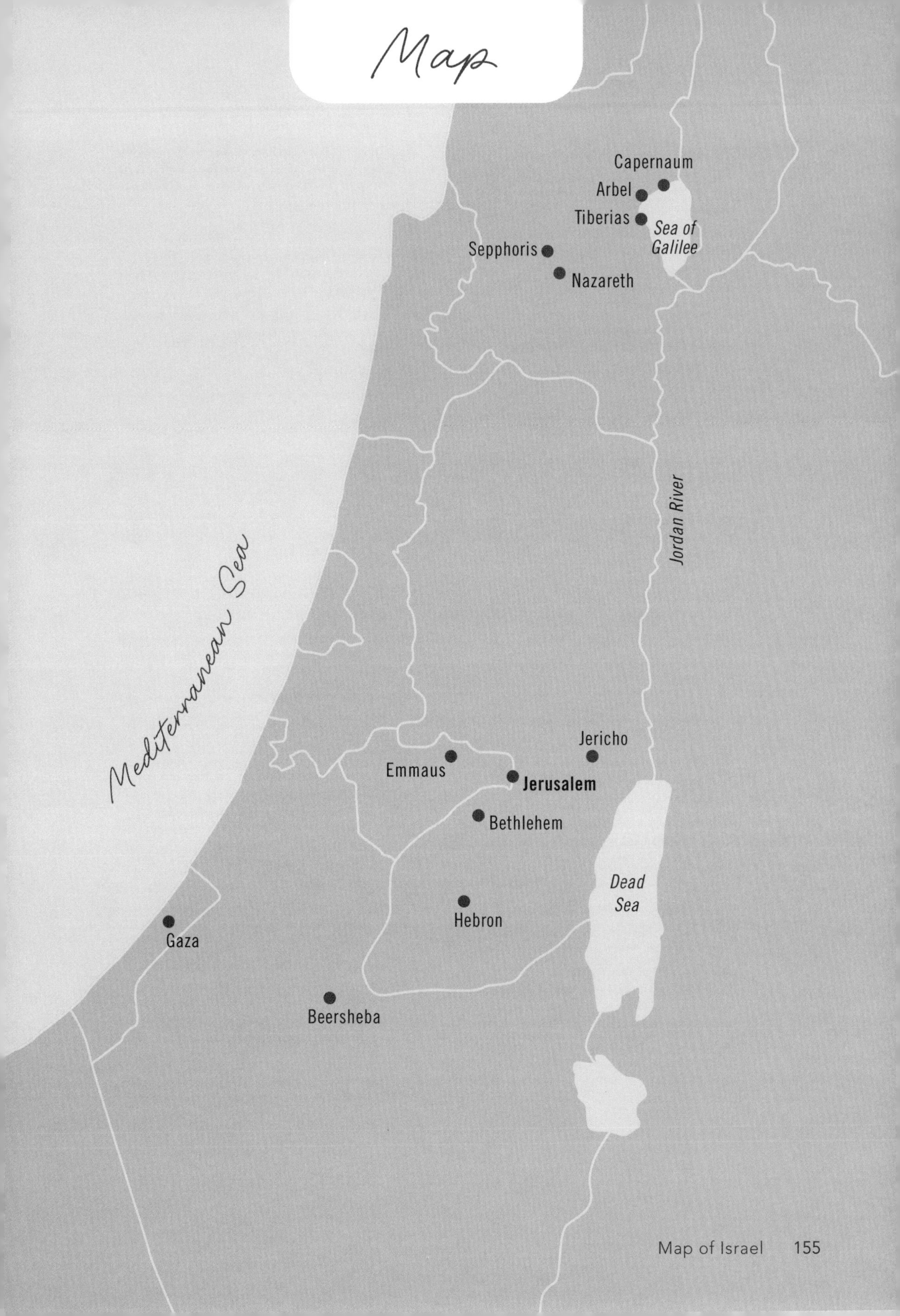
Capernaum
Arbel
Tiberias
Sea of Galilee
Sepphoris
Nazareth
Jordan River
Mediterranean Sea
Jericho
Emmaus
Jerusalem
Bethlehem
Dead Sea
Hebron
Gaza
Beersheba

Endnotes

SESSION ONE

1. W. John Burghardt, "St. Jerome," *Encyclopedia Britannica*, accessed March 15, 2024, https://www.britannica.com/biography/Saint-Jerome.

2. Don Stewart, "Why Is the Bible Divided into Chapters and Verses?," *Blue Letter Bible*, accessed October 10, 2023, https://www.blueletterbible.org/Comm/stewart_don/faq/bible-special/question8-why-is-the-bible-divided-into-chapters-and-verses.cfm.

3. "Introduction to the Gospel of Luke," *Blue Letter Bible*, accessed March 21, 2024, https://www.blueletterbible.org/study/intros/luke.cfm.

4. Ibid.

5. Frank E. Dicken, "Luke," *The Lexham Bible Dictionary*, ed. John D. Barry et al. (Bellingham, WA: Lexham Press, 2016).

6. Flavius, Josephus, *Against Apion* (Germany: Books on Demand, 2019).

7. Alan J. Thompson, "Acts: A Commentary," *The Gospel Coalition*, accessed March 22, 2024, https://www.thegospelcoalition.org/commentary/acts/#section-1.

8. "Detailed Intertestamental Timeline with Notes on Judaism," *BibleHistory.com*, accessed March 22, 2024, https://bible-history.com/resource/timeline-with-notes-on-judaism-400-165-bc.

9. Kieren Johns, "The Roman-Jewish Wars: Jewish Resistance vs Roman Might," *The Collector*, December 20, 2023, https://www.thecollector.com/roman-jewish-wars-history/.

10. "Battle of Pharsalus summary," *Encyclopedia Britannica*, April 29, 2021, https://www.britannica.com/summary/Battle-of-Pharsalus.

11. M. Grant, "Augustus," *Encyclopedia Britannica*, February 13, 2024, https://www.britannica.com/biography/Augustus-Roman-emperor.

12. "Son of God," *New World Encyclopedia*, February 23, 2023, https://www.newworldencyclopedia.org/entry/Son_of_God.

13. "Pax Romana," *Encyclopedia Britannica*, February 23, 2024, https://www.britannica.com/event/Pax-Romana.

14. S. Henry Perowne, "Herod," *Encyclopedia Britannica*, March 12, 2024, https://www.britannica.com/biography/Herod-king-of-Judaea.

15. Don Stewart, "Who Were the Herods?," *Blue Letter Bible*, June 9, 2020, https://www.blueletterbible.org/Comm/stewart_don/faq/the-world-into-which-jesus-came/06-who-were-the-herods.cfm.

16. Placide Cappeau, "O holy night the stars are brightly shining," trans. John S. Dwight (1847).

17. "Strong's G4990," *Blue Letter Bible*, accessed March 22, 2024, https://www.blueletterbible.org/lexicon/g4990/kjv/tr/0-1/.

18. Dwight A. Pryor, *Unveiling the Kingdom of Heaven: The Origins and Dimensions of the Kingdom Concept as Taught by the Rabbi Jesus* (Center for Judaic-Christian Studies, 2008), Introduction, ix.

19. Ibid, 16.

20. Stanley J. Grenz, David Guretzki, Cherith Fee Nordling, *Pocket Dictionary of Theological Terms* (United Kingdom: InterVarsity Press, 2010), 71.

21. "Advent," *Encyclopedia Britannica*, March 6, 2024, https://www.britannica.com/topic/Advent.

22. "The Lord's Most Tender Inquiry," *Israel Institute of Biblical Studies*, accessed March 22, 2024, https://lp.israelbiblicalstudies.com/lp-iibs-biblical-hebrew-knowing-an-hebrew-verse-en.html.

SESSION TWO

1. James, *The Protoevangelium of James*, trans. Lily C. Vuong (Eugene, OR: Cascade Books), 9:2.

2. *The Mishnah: Translated from the Hebrew with Introduction and Brief Explanatory Notes* (United States: Hendrickson Publishers, 2011), Ketubbot 5:2.

3. "Strong's G5045," *Blue Letter Bible*, accessed March 22, 2024, https://www.blueletterbible.org/lexicon/g5045/niv/mgnt/0-1/.

4. "Gospel of James," *New World Encylcopedia*, accessed April 2, 2024, https://www.newworldencyclopedia.org/entry/Gospel_of_James.

5. "Strong's G1342," *Blue Letter Bible*, accessed March 22, 2024, https://www.blueletterbible.org/lexicon/g1342/niv/mgnt/0-1/.

6. Maria Peña, "The Ketubah, An Ornate Jewish Marriage Tradition," *The Library of Congress*, June 9, 2023, https://blogs.loc.gov/loc/2023/06/the-ketubah-an-ornate-jewish-marriage-tradition/.

7. Ibid.

8. *The Mishnah*, Kettubot 5:2.

9. *The Babylonian Talmud: Translated into English for the First Time, with Introduction, Commentary, Glossary and Indices*, trans. Abraham Cohen (Cambridge University Press, 2013), Pesachim 113a.

10. Michael Zank, "The Rabbinic Epithet Gevurah," in *Approaches to Ancient Judaism*, 1998, vol. xiv, accessed March 22, 2024, https://www.bu.edu/mzank/Michael_Zank/gevurah.html#:~:text=Literally%2C%20and%20in%20its%20biblical,%22effeminate%22%20appearance%20of%20weakness.

11. Todd Bolen, "Sepphoris," *BiblePlaces.com*, accessed March 22, 2024, https://www.bibleplaces.com/templemount/.

12. Dale Cockrell, "The Music Pa Ingalls Played," *HUMANITIES*, Spring 2020, vol. 41.2, accessed March 22, 2024, https://www.neh.gov/article/music-pa-ingalls-played#:~:text=%E2%80%9CLet%20me%20make%20the%20songs,Scotland%2C%20English%20political%20machinations%20notwithstanding.

13. "Strong's G2098," *Blue Letter Bible*, accessed March 22, 2024, https://www.blueletterbible.org/lexicon/g2098/esv/tr/0-1/.

14. Russ Ramsey, "Where the Lambs Are Kept: A Narrative Retelling of Luke 2:8–15," *The Gospel Coalition*, December 23, 2015, https://www.thegospelcoalition.org/article/where-the-lambs-are-kept/.

15. Dr. Juergen Buehler, "The Tower of the Flock," *International Christian Embassy Jerusalem*, November 22, 2012, https://www.icej.org/blog/the-tower-of-the-flock/.

16. "The Shepherd's Field," *Bethlehem University*, accessed March 22, 2024, https://www.bethlehem.edu/2020/03/02/the-shepherds-field/.

17. "A.D. 70 Titus Destroys Jerusalem," *Christianity Today*, accessed April 2, 2024, https://www.christianitytoday.com/history/issues/issue-28/ad-70-titus-destroys-jerusalem.html.

18. "Strong's G2097," *Blue Letter Bible*, accessed March 22, 2024, https://www.blueletterbible.org/lexicon/g2097/esv/tr/0-1/.

19. "Strong's H8615," *Blue Letter Bible*, accessed March 22, 2024, https://www.blueletterbible.org/lexicon/h8615/kjv/wlc/0-1/.

20. Ibid.

SESSION THREE

1. A. Boyd Luter, "Luke," in *CSB Study Bible: Notes*, ed. Edwin A. Blum and Trevin Wax (Nashville, TN: Holman Bible Publishers, 2017), 1609.

2. Everett Ferguson, *Baptism in the Early Church* (Grand Rapids, MI: Eerdmans Publishing Company, 2009).

3. Rabbi Jonathan Sacks, "The Wilderness and the Word," *Jonathan Sacks: The Rabbi Sacks Legacy,* accessed October 20, 2023, https://www.rabbisacks.org/covenant-conversation/bamidbar/the-wilderness-and-the-word/.

4. "Strong's H1980," *Blue Letter Bible*, accessed March 22, 2024, https://www.blueletterbible.org/lexicon/h1980/kjv/wlc/0-1/.

5. Fr. Wade Menezes, "The Significance of 40 in Sacred Scripture," *The Fathers of Mercy*, accessed March 22, 2024, https://fathersofmercy.com/the-significance-of-40-in-scripture/#:~:text=In%20Sacred%20Scripture%2C%20the%20number,lasted%2040%20days%20and%20nights.

6. R. C. Sproul, "Jesus in the Synagogue," sermon transcript, *Ligonier Ministries*, March 25, 2012, https://www.ligonier.org/learn/sermons/jesus-synagogue.

7. "Derasha," *Encyclopedia Britannica*, February 15, 2016, https://www.britannica.com/topic/derasha.

8. "Strong's H5342," *Blue Letter Bible*, accessed March 22, 2024, https://www.blueletterbible.org/lexicon/h5342/kjv/wlc/0-1/.

9. *The Mishnah*, Sotah 3:8, Sanhedrin 6:4.

10. John J. Parsons, "Baiyt—House," *Hebrew for Christians*, accessed March 22, 2024, https://www.hebrew4christians.com/Glossary/Word_of_the_Week/Archived/Bayit/bayit.html.

SESSION FOUR

1. "Kinneret - Sea of Galilee," *The Israel Forever Foundation*, accessed March 22, 2024, https://israelforever.org/israel/exploring/the_kinneret/.

2. "Am-ha-aretz," *Encyclopedia Britannica*, accessed March 22, 2024, https://www.britannica.com/topic/am-ha-aretz.

3. "Strong's H7227," *Blue Letter Bible*, accessed March 25, 2024, https://www.blueletterbible.org/lexicon/h7227/niv/wlc/0-1/.

4. C. S. Lewis, *The Last Battle: The Classic Fantasy Adventure Series* (Official Edition) (United Kingdom: HarperCollins, 2009).

5. *NIV First-Century Study Bible: Explore Scripture in Its Jewish and Early Christian Context* (United States: Zondervan, 2014), 1374-1375.

6. Mark Batterson, *The Circle Maker: Praying Circles Around Your Biggest Dreams and Greatest Fears* (United States: Zondervan, 2016), 11.

7. Levi Cooper, "World Of The Sages: Unique Contributions," *The Jerusalem Post*, July 11, 2007, https://www.jpost.com/jewish-world/judaism/world-of-the-sages-unique-contributions.

8. Ron Mosely, *Yeshua: A Guide to the Real Jesus and the Original Church* (Messianic Jewish Publishers, 1998), 121-124.

9. *The International Standard Bible Encyclopedia New and Revised Edition*, ed. Melvin Grove Kyle (Chicago: Eerdmans Publishing).

10. *The Mishnah*, Sanhedrin, 25b.15, 16.

11. *The Babylonian Talmud*, Bava Kamma 113a.

12. *The Mishnah*, Bava Kamma 10, Nedarim 3.4, 27b-28a.

13. "Strong's H7673," *Blue Letter Bible*, accessed March 25, 2024, https://www.blueletterbible.org/lexicon/h7673/kjv/wlc/0-1/.

14. Dr. Paul H. Wright, *Rose Guide to the Feasts, Festivals and Fasts of the Bible* (United States: Rose Publishing, 2022), 79-80.

15. *The Mishnah*, Yoma 8:6.

16. "Mishnah on Saving Life on Sabbath," *NIV First-Century Study Bible*, 1211-12, 1252, 1655.

17. "Shabbat: An Island in Time," *Chabad.org*, accessed March 22, 2024, https://www.chabad.org/library/article_cdo/aid/253215/jewish/Shabbat.htm.

SESSION FIVE

1. Lewis.
2. Douglas S. Huffman, "Gospel of Luke," in *The Lexham Bible Dictionary*.
3. James R. Edwards, "The Gospel according to Luke," in *The Pillar New Testament Commentary*, ed. D. A. Carson (Grand Rapids, MI: Eerdmans, 2015), 302.
4. *The Mishnah*, Berakoth 9:5.
5. Rabbi Geoffry Dennis, "Jewish Exorcism," *MyJewishLearning.com*, accessed March 22, 2024, https://www.myjewishlearning.com/article/jewish-exorcism/.
6. *NIV First-Century Study Bible*, 1256.
7. A. W. Tozer, *The Pursuit of God*, ebook (Perlego, 2008), 16.
8. "Generosity Liturgy," *NYC Church of the City*, accessed March 22, 2024, https://www.church.nyc/give.
9. Abraham Joshua Heschel, *The Sabbath* (United States: Farrar, Straus and Giroux, 2005), 54.
10. "Strong's H4496," *Blue Letter Bible*, accessed March 25, 2024, https://www.blueletterbible.org/lexicon/h4496/kjv/wlc/0-1.
11. Heschel, 14.
12. Ibid., 66.

SESSION SIX

1. David S. Dockery, ed., *Holman Bible Handbook* (Nashville, TN: Holman Bible Publishers, 1992), 619.
2. "Strong's G2646," *Blue Letter Bible*, accessed March 25, 2024, https://www.blueletterbible.org/lexicon/g2646/kjv/tr/0-1/.
3. Marcus Tullius Cicero, *Against Verres* (Czechia: DigiCat, 2023), 2.5.165; 2.5.168
4. Barry Strauss, *The Spartacus War* (United States: Simon & Schuster, 2009), 189-195.
5. Ibid.
6. Ibid.
7. "Church of the Holy Sepulchre," *HolyLandSite.com*, accessed March 25, 2024, https://www.holylandsite.com/church-of-the-holy-sepulchre.
8. "Golgotha," *Encyclopedia Britannica*, February 22, 2024, https://www.britannica.com/place/Golgotha.
9. "Tamid," *The Jewish Virtual Library*, accessed March 25, 2024, https://www.jewishvirtuallibrary.org/tamid.
10. *The Mishnah*, Shekalim, 8:5.

SESSION SEVEN

1. Jessica da Costa Minati Moraes, "Helena of Constantinople," *World History Encyclopedia*, April 21, 2022, https://www.worldhistory.org/Helena_of_Constantinople/.
2. "Biblical Israel: First-Century Tombs and Burial," *CBNIsrael.org*, February 8, 2022, https://cbnisrael.org/2022/02/08/biblical-israel-first-century-tombs-and-burial-2/.
3. Dr. Ron Moseley, *Yeshua: A Guide to the Real Jesus and the Original Church* (United States: Messianic Jewish Publishers, 1998), 123-124.
4. "Strong's G3093," *Blue Letter Bible*, accessed March 25, 2024, https://www.blueletterbible.org/lexicon/g3093/kjv/tr/0-1/.
5. Rabbi Reuven P. Bulka, *Fixing Tikkun Olam & Other Essays* (United States: Ahavat Shalom Publishers, 2021), 45-61.
6. Lewis.

Get the most from your study.

Customize your Bible study time with a guided experience.

In this study, you'll:

· Travel through Israel to the places Jesus walked to behold the gospel story in a whole new way.

· Gain a deeper understanding of common stories retold from a first-century point of view.

· Explore cultural and historical concepts that will give new perspective on well-known biblical stories.

STUDYING ON YOUR OWN?

Watch Kristi McLelland's teaching sessions, available via redemption code for individual video-streaming access, printed in this Bible study book.

LEADING A GROUP?

Each group member will need a *Luke in the Land* Bible study book, which includes video access. Because all participants will have access to the video content, you can choose to watch the videos outside of your group meeting if desired. Or, if you're watching together and someone misses a group meeting, they'll have the flexibility to catch up! A DVD set is also available to purchase separately if desired.

ADDITIONAL RESOURCES

DVD Set, includes 7 video teaching sessions from Kristi McLelland, each approximately 35–45 minutes.

eBook with video access, includes 7 video teaching sessions from Kristi McLelland, each approximately 35–45 minutes.

Browse study formats, a free session sample, video clips, church promotional materials, and more at

lifeway.com/lukeintheland

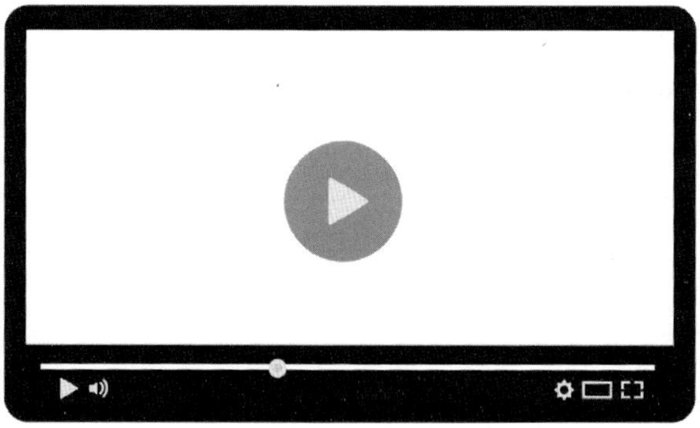

HERE'S YOUR VIDEO ACCESS.

To stream *Luke in the Land* Bible study video teaching sessions, follow these steps:

1. Go to my.lifeway.com/redeem and register or log in to your Lifeway account.

2. Enter this redemption code to gain access to your individual-use video license:

BMCDQKM9S8YX

Once you've entered your personal redemption code, you can stream the video teaching sessions any time from your Digital Media page on my.lifeway.com or watch them via the Lifeway On Demand app on any TV or mobile device via your Lifeway account.

There's no need to enter your code more than once! To watch your streaming videos, just log in to your Lifeway account at my.lifeway.com or watch using the Lifeway On Demand app.

QUESTIONS? WE HAVE ANSWERS!
Visit support.lifeway.com and search "Video Redemption Code" or call our Tech Support Team at 866.627.8553.